THE SHOOTING SCRIPT

JUDE

SCREENPLAY AND INTRODUCTION BY
HOSSEIN AMINI

The NHB Shooting Script Series

NICK HERN BOOKS
LONDON

To Alexandra and Nina

Introduction copyright © 1996 Hossein Amini
Screenplay copyright © 1996 PolyGram Films (UK) Ltd
Photography by Joss Barratt copyright © PolyGram Film Productions BV
Published by arrangement with Macmillan Publishers Ltd

The Shooting Script Series was originally devised by Newmarket Press
The Newmarket Shooting Script Series is a registered trademark of Newmarket Press,
a division of Newmarket Publishing & Communications Corporation

This book first published in Great Britain in 1996
as an original paperback by
Nick Hern Books Ltd, 14 Larden Road, London W3 7ST.

A CIP catalogue for this book is available from the British Library.

ISBN 1 85459 302 1

Introduction and prelims typeset by Country Setting
Woodchurch, Kent TN26 3TB
Printed and bound in Great Britain by Hobbs the Printers Ltd
Totton, Hants. S040 3YS

THE NHB SHOOTING SCRIPT SERIES

The Age of Innocence
The Birdcage
The Ice Storm
Jude
The People vs. Larry Flynt
The Shawshank Redemption

For information on forthcoming titles, please contact the publishers:
NHB, 14 Larden Road, London W3 7ST

THE JUDE SCREENPLAY
A PERSONAL ACCOUNT

Have you ever read *Jude the Obscure*? Nick Marston my agent asked. 'Yes,' I lied. 'Did you like it?' 'I can't really remember it. I read it at school.' 'Do you know Michael Winterbottom's work?' 'Yes,' I lied again. 'Do you like it?', 'Of course.' A few days later when I met Michael Winterbottom and the producer Andrew Eaton for the first time I still hadn't finished the book. They kept talking about 'the scene with the children', and I improvised, hoping they wouldn't find me out. I was desperate to write a movie, any movie.

I wish I could say *Jude* was the book I'd always wanted to adapt, but it wasn't. I'd only ever been commissioned to write for television before, and *Jude* was the first and only feature film script I was offered. I didn't even like the book much the first time I read it. I admired it intellectually, but it seemed so far away from my own experiences. Jude was a stonemason who couldn't get into Christminster University because of his class; I'd been to an English private school and spent three years at Oxford because of my privileged background. Here was an epic drama about the English class system, and I wasn't even English. And then there was the love story: a man who gave up all his dreams for the love of a woman. Noble sentiments but so far away from my own on/off relationships conducted in the shadow of an unwavering career ambition.

Or so I thought.

A short time later my girlfriend of three months became pregnant, and my ordered universe threatened to collapse around me. All the opportunities and rewards I'd day-dreamed for the last ten years suddenly seemed utterly out of reach. I was going to have to earn proper money, take care of a child, and sacrifice all my precious plans. In retrospect all this seems overdramatic, but at the time that was how I felt. Suddenly the famous passage in the book where Jude watches the scholars' parade at Christminster made resonant sense to me:

'Eight or nine years ago when I came here first, I had a neat stock of fixed opinions, but they dropped away one by one; and the further I get the less sure I am . . . "For who knoweth what is good for man in this life? And who can tell a man what shall be after him under the sun."'

This passage became the key to my adaptation. Its theme was vast and universal and yet it struck a deeply personal chord. We set out from small confines, with clear ideals, and carefully laid plans for the future, and then suddenly, events or people beyond our control sweep us away in a completely different direction.

The second time I read *Jude the Obscure* I lost myself in it completely. I didn't read it like books I'd read at school or university. There was no objectivity, no detachment. I clung to the ideas that made sense to me emotionally and skimmed over passages that I couldn't relate to. I'm sure I would have failed an exam on the book because I was already re-imagining it in my head. That's how I read books I love, and that's the only way I know how to adapt them. However arrogant it sounds I had to try to make the book my own. It's an easier task with books no-one's heard of or nobody likes. The problem with *Jude the Obscure* is that a great many people have read it in the way I read it, intimately, passionately, and with their own unique picture of the characters, the landscape, and the ideas.

I could have gone to talk to Hardy experts, or researched the critical writings on the book, but rightly or wrongly I chose not to. I wanted to write the script as I'd read the novel. On my own. As privately and personally as I could. I wanted to try to capture the emotions I felt when I turned the last page and sat back to reflect.

What I didn't realise at the time was that it doesn't work like this in the Film Industry. Even at the script stage there is something called a Director.

If there was anyone who challenged my personal claim on Hardy's last novel it was Michael Winterbottom. It was his favourite book. Ever. He'd even filmed the pig killing scene as his student exercise at film school.

At our first script meeting, before I'd written a word, Michael made it clear that he saw the book as a love story between Jude and Sue. Although he didn't say it straight out, he implied he wanted to end the film with the two lovers parting.

And leave out Jude's death, I thought to myself. Impossible. I went away knowing I had the book to myself for three months with no interference from any-one. I'd write such an intense death scene that Michael would readily change his mind.

The writing, however, was not uninterrupted. Firstly on the domestic front the tensions of an unplanned pregnancy flared frequently. Alex, my girlfriend, couldn't decide if she was ready to commit to me and life with a baby. After all we'd only known each other a few months. We argued incessantly. I was constantly afraid she'd change her mind about keeping the baby. For the first time in my life I felt that my future and my emotional balance were in someone else's hands.

I escaped to my study and wrote to distract myself. Even then I'd find a lot of my conversations with Alex creeping into the script. Few of them survived the final draft, but they informed almost all of the relationships. Jude and Sue, Jude and Arabella, Sue and Phillotson, all became warring couples at each other's throats.

Even though it was an adaptation, this script was turning into the most personal thing I'd ever written. Thirty pages into the first draft I suddenly lost all confidence. It was coming to me too easily, too quickly, perhaps too personally. I phoned Andrew Eaton, and asked him if he'd have a look at the first few pages, just in case I was going horribly wrong. A few hours later he phoned back to say it was fine, but that Michael had a few points. My heart sunk. He was going to tell me I was drifting too far from the book.

Michael called and told me I was sticking too closely to the book. He liked the fact that the dialogue had a contemporary feel to it, but that I could still go considerably further.

I completed my first draft in seven weeks, which is very fast for me. The scene I was proudest of was Jude's death scene. As in the book, I had him in a small room, listening to the sounds of the Christminster parade outside, still clinging to the University dream that had eluded him. The triumph of the indomitable human spirit. As he died we'd move out of his window and follow the jubilant crowds down to the river, more and more of them joining the ebb and flow, a great human tidal wave moving ever forwards...

Michael didn't like it. He thought my ending worked but it wasn't what he wanted to say in the film. He wanted the film to end with the lovers parting. He wanted to avoid melodrama and forced sentimentality. What he had always loved about the book was its emotional honesty, how real the tragedy felt, extreme at times, but also beautifully simple and understated. My ending suddenly felt arch and flabby. I went away to re-write.

I was equally proud of my second ending. Given the limitation that I couldn't show Jude dying, I was determined to at least imply it. My second draft ending went something like this. Jude is sick in bed. A Doctor examines him and tells him he must rest. Jude knows he's dying, but he has to see Sue one last time. He sets off after her. We see him taking the train. We see him walking across rainswept fields. All familiar images we have seen before, now seen in a different light, the inevitability of his fall echoing from the beginning. Jude finds Sue, and their final parting scene is played under the shelter of a tree, with the rain shutting them off from the rest of the world.

Again Michael didn't like it. There was no need to see Jude travelling to Sue. They should just meet at the graveyard where their children are buried. And part. This time I argued my case more vociferously. Without the heroism of Jude's search for Sue, the ending would be intolerably bleak and matter of fact. The audience wouldn't know how they were supposed to feel. What was wrong with that, Michael argued, it was emotionally more real, and honest. For the first and only time we hit an 'impasse' on the script. I was nervous about audience expectations, Michael was determined to see through his vision. He won, and in retrospect he was probably right, although I didn't think so at the time. I went away chastened and frightened by the Director's ultimate power over the screenplay. It turned out to be a good thing. Michael Winterbottom didn't write a word of the screenplay, but his stamp was all over it. A good Director directs the writer in the same way he directs the actors. I adjusted to Michael's style, sometimes reluctantly, but in the end I took a great deal of it away with me.

I handed in the second draft of *Jude* to Mark Shivas, head of BBC Films, in April of 1995, five months after I'd first started working on the project. Alex and I were getting on by now and we went away to Spain together for our last holiday before the baby was born.

On holiday I tried to put the script out of my head, but I couldn't. This was the first real moment of truth. As a writer starting out I had spent the whole time thinking, Oh God, when will someone pay me to write a script? and then as a working writer I kept thinking, Oh God, when will someone make my script? I had spent almost two years writing a four part mini-series for the BBC that never got made. It broke my heart and my confidence. Deep down I never thought *Jude* would get made. I was already bracing myself for disappointment.

Mark Shivas liked the script. He was prepared to put in £800,000 towards the film, the BBC maximum, and also to put his weight behind finding the rest of the money from prospective co-producers. With this encouragement I set about polishing the script in preparation for the Cannes Film Market, where Andrew and Michael and Mark would submit it for consideration. I wasn't entirely hopeful, not because I didn't believe in the script, but because the likelihood of anything getting made was always so slim. When Andrew didn't ring immediately I assumed the worst. I prepared myself for another two years of anxious waiting, with trickles of optimistic news that never led to anything.

I always get my good news on answer machines. When I phone up and ask, the reply is usually negative, so I superstitiously resisted calling Andrew and waited it out. A week later he called and told me not to get too excited, but it looked like Polygram might fund the film. I examined every nuance in his voice but couldn't get anything more definite. What percentage chance, I finally asked him. About ninety-nine he replied.

That was good enough for me. I phoned all my friends and told them the film had been greenlighted, and dropped in the fact that it was being made for Polygram

Filmed Entertainment, the distributors of *Four Weddings and a Funeral*, as if by association alone my film would be equally successful. Everywhere I went I bragged.

And then the one percent started to haunt me. What if Polygram didn't want to fund the film after all. I felt like phoning up everyone I'd talked to and qualifying my idle boasts. At my wedding, my best man toasted the upcoming production of my first feature film, and everyone raised a glass. I smiled nervously and kept thinking to myself what if it all folds.

There was never one moment when the film was definitely on. It was a series of stages, none of them an absolute confirmation, and more worryingly, none of them irrevocable. I pestered Andrew Eaton incessantly. Have you exchanged contracts with Polygram? Is the money in the bank? Can they still change their minds?

Pre-production begun in July. All I could think was that Polygram still had August, September, and October to change their minds.

I think my first visit to the *Jude* Production Office was the moment I really thought the film might get made. For a start there were a dozen people working in the building. All of them must have been getting paid something, so I was reassured that Polygram had started spending money. And then there were the costumes and the location photographs. I was thrilled to see my scene descriptions coming to life so vividly, but I was more thrilled to know location managers and designers were also on the payroll. My most comforting moment however came when I saw Christopher Eccleston's photograph pinned to a drawing board. For the first time I felt certain the film was going to get made.

I turned up at the Production Office as often as I could. Rather than faxing through re-writes I'd deliver them by hand. Everyone was accommodating, but it didn't take me long to realise I was in the way. Every minute showing me around the various departments was a minute wasted. My job had finished, and everyone else's had begun. The script was no longer my private property; it had become a fully operational working tool for other people. The Designers, the Cinematographer, the Locations Manager, everyone looked through it briefly, and then set about refining it for their own needs.

The only further work I was required to do was to adjust the screenplay to suit those needs. The Locations Manager had found a stunning Victorian hot house so the art gallery scene in Melchester became the hot house scene. It was expensive to build a fairground House of Horror, so the Tunnel of Doom turned into a magic lantern show. Almost imperceptibly the script was changing. I waited anxiously for the moment when the actors would come in, and I would have to make the same adjustments to the dialogue.

The day of the readthrough I nervously introduced myself to our Jude and Sue, Chris Eccleston and Kate Winslet. Neither of them suggested any drastic changes.

I thought I'd got away with it, when Rachel Griffiths who was playing the part of Arabella took me aside to discuss her lines. I had often read about actors who demanded vast chunks of dialogue be added or rewritten for them so I feared the worst. I was completely unprepared for the lesson in screenwriting brevity I was about to get from Rachel. She took me through all the superfluous lines I had written for her and suggested we get rid of all of them. She was right, and it was all the more admirable because she didn't have that many lines to start with. She also suggested I map out Arabella's story during the time she was away from the main narrative. Though none of this backstory was ever used directly, it helped inform her character throughout.

The read through itself was over very quickly. I don't write much dialogue, so the whole thing sounded like a sparse Pinteresque exercise. Without the descriptions there didn't seem to be much left. I said goodbye to everyone and wished them luck and waited anxiously for the first day's rushes.

From the moment I saw the first take I had an overall sense of what the film would look like. It was much starker than I had expected, and much grander. In all the shots the characters seemed dwarfed by the epic landscape. I was thrilled by the scale and ambition of the imagery, but worried that my dialogue would be completely overpowered. My words seemed trite. The pictures and silences said so much more. I felt my script was completely unworthy of this film.

I was reassured when I saw the first few scenes between Jude and Sue. There was a naturalism in the performances that I'd never seen before in period films. It reflected perfectly the sparse everyday dialogue I'd tried to write. For the first time I could see my own imprint on the film, and it seemed to be working. None of my dialogue made me cringe, which was a first. The actors' rhythm, their timing, their stresses, and pauses, everything was identical to how I'd heard it in my head when I wrote it. I completely trusted Michael and his cast now. I didn't ask to see any more rushes after that. I got on with the rest of my life and waited three months to see the first cut of the film.

*

I was horribly nervous on the day of the screening. My previous experiences watching TV films I had written for the first time had always been disappointing. I warned my wife that I might come back with an inconsolable depression, and if I did would she please bear with me.

I can't remember fully what I went through for the next two hours, but it was a series of absolute highs, and absolute lows. I knew the film was going to be very different from the film in my head, but every scene or line of mine that had been cut went through me like a knife. When a sequence didn't seem to be working I felt a terrible rush of anxiety. When the film dragged I slouched in my seat, and despaired. It usually took me two or three scenes to recover from a disappointment, but I always recovered in the end. There were many more highs than lows. I felt a rush of energy every time a scene or a moment delivered. I remember some of them vividly: Jude's wedding; the moment he faces down the crowd in the pub and recites the credo in Latin; the exchange between Jude and Sue as they walk along the riverbank; and my very favourite moment, when Sue is dressed in Jude's clothes, sitting on his armchair by the fire, waiting for him to kiss her.

Slowly I started to watch the film as a film, divorced from my own ideas of how it should have been made, and divorced from my anxieties about its eventual success. By the end I was sure we had something special. For the first time in my writing career I felt I was involved in something I could be proud of. But there was also something sad about the experience. Perhaps it was the realisation that the film that was in my head was never going to be completed. I read somewhere that the screenplay is the dream of the finished film. The finished film thrilled me beyond all expectations, but a part of me mourned the screenplay that had vanished.

I didn't take long to get over it. More people saw the film, and they seemed unanimously positive. My dreams were starting to get ahead of me again. Like everyone else I was certain we were going to get into competition at the Cannes Film Festival. A part of me even thought we might win something.

It was a real shock when Gilles Jacob, the Director of the competition section of the Cannes Festival turned *Jude* down. I was despondent. It wasn't just the fact that all those unspoken hopes of a Palme D'Or had suddenly vanished, it was more the fact that finally someone had seen the film and not liked it. The following week the Director's Fortnight Selectors saw the film and chose it without hesitation, but somehow that air of invulnerability had gone. I suppose this must be a feeling that every first time filmmaker goes through, the moment when you realise there are going to be some people who don't like your work no matter how perfect you think it is. I still didn't think there would be many dissenters. This feeling was reinforced when the Daily Mail gave us a rave review after the first pre-Cannes press screening. The feeling of elation only lasted a day. The following morning the Daily Telegraph called *Jude* a fair stab at Hardy's masterpiece. The mixed reviews had started.

Suddenly I became nervous about the screening at Cannes. My wife was going to be there, and so was my inordinately proud father. I'd heard that films were somtimes booed at festivals. The idea of my poor dad having to sit through cat-calls filled me with dread.

I didn't have the courage to go to the morning press screening at Cannes, but I heard we got a standing ovation. With a new found confidence I attended the press conference, and once again the journalists seemed to be mostly upbeat about the film. I was finally looking forward to the gala screening that night.

The film dragged interminably. Every cough, and every shuffle from the audience made me panic. For the first time I saw faults I had never seen before. As the lights went up again I feared the worst.

Suddenly everyone was on their feet, and I found myself being called onto the stage alongside Andrew, Michael, and the cast. The standing ovation went on and on. I looked at Andrew, and he had tears in his eyes. It was the one moment I felt nothing could go wrong, and although I didn't know it at the time, it was the moment everything started going downwards.

The backlash started the next day. There were rumours that some of the British press hadn't liked the film. They were all critics I had read and admired as a film buff. I tried to reconcile my passion for the film with my respect for their opinions. I couldn't. I invariably blamed my own writing. It was the beginning of a process that would go on for months. Every good review I read, I'd flick through and forget. Every bad review I'd re-read several times and involuntarily memorise.

I remember the first time I met with Michael and Andrew to discuss the adaptation of *Jude*, we had jokingly anticipated the hostility of the critics to the 'modern' approach we were going to take. We felt bullish at the time: provocative, uncompromising. It's easy when you're sitting in a pub in Soho, dreaming up plans in isolation. I don't think any of us realised how vulnerable we'd be feeling two years later when the first reviews came in. I for one didn't. I found myself running to the local newsagents scouring every magazine for some verdict on our film. For the entire summer I anticipated, and blew out of all proportion, the critical battering I thought *Jude* would get.

In the meantime there was some good news too. *Jude* won first prize at the Edinburgh and Dinard film festivals; and the reputation it was building up on the festival circuit got me some nice work offers. Some of the American producers who had seen the film at Cannes got in touch with me to tell me how much they had liked it. They also allayed my worst fears by telling me that it was completely normal to get mixed reviews with this sort of film. If you were going to treat a difficult subject in a provocative way, you were bound to get a mixed reaction, you almost wanted it.

I told myself they were right. I kept trying to remind myself that many of the great films had got a critical battering when they first came out. But then so had the really bad ones. I was incredibly jealous when *Secrets and Lies* came out in the summer to unanimously great reviews.

When the moment of truth came my nerve failed me. I deliberately timed a work trip to Los Angeles to coincide with the opening of *Jude* in London. I couldn't bear to read the newspaper reviews, but I knew I wouldn't be able to resist going down to my local newsagent and buying every single one of them. It was safer to be abroad, away from temptation. I didn't realise all the British papers would be available in the lobby of my hotel in Los Angeles.

I read a few of them. The good ones I flicked through, the bad ones I took to heart. Occasionally I felt indignant. As the writer I was being singled out and blamed for things that were sometimes completely out of my hands; decisions that weren't even mine in the first place. The worst side of my nature blamed Michael for downplaying the romanticism of the script, cutting long sections and link scenes out, adding chapter headings, changing my original ending, but the more faithful part of me remembered how many of the ideas in the script were his, and how grateful I was to him when the lights went up after the first screening. My first instincts when I saw *Jude* were that this was a great film and this was a fine director. That was before anyone else had seen it, or anyone had written about it.

Jude opened on October 4th in London and had a very respectable opening weekend. My dream had always been to watch a film I'd written in a real cinema with a paying audience, but once again at the last moment my nerve failed me. I went to see another film at the same cinema where *Jude* was showing. I had a quick look in the *Jude* theatre to see if there was anyone there. To my relief it was almost three quarters full, not quite a triumph, but certainly not embarrassing.

Two weeks later the film opened in the United States to some very good reviews. I eagerly awaited the first weekend's box office results. I even read a few of the film finance magazines so I'd have some understanding of what the figures meant. In the event I didn't need to. Andrew Eaton phoned me up on the Saturday night saying that *Jude* hadn't performed as well as we had hoped. We'd failed the most important test.

That weekend was the lowest point for me. Reviews meant nothing when nobody was going to see the film. I thought back to Cannes and the enormous expectations we all had for ourselves and the film. That weekend was the culmination of a downward slide that had been going on all summer. This was my first film on the big screen, and when it finally came round I couldn't enjoy a moment of it. I tried to tell myself that it was a wonderful privilege to have something I'd written be produced, and shown in a cinema, but of course that wasn't enough anymore. I'd set myself new boundaries, and dreamed new dreams, and the film wasn't going to deliver any of them.

Luckily the phone rang a few times that weekend. People called me from Los Angeles to tell me how much they'd enjoyed the film. Others faxed through the good reviews we'd had. My agents gave me a much needed dose of realism. What had I expected? The film was trying to break into an incredibly competitive market, at an incredibly competitive time. The Box Office results were respectable and, given the nature of the material, hardly surprising. The film had achieved what it had set out to do. It was brave and difficult and different, and I should be proud of it.

I bought an American newspaper the next day, and flicked through the entertainment section. There were about forty illustrated adverts for different films showing, and *Jude* was only one of them. It didn't even have a very prominent advert. For me *Jude* had been the most important film in the world, but at the end of the day it was only one amongst many. Every screenwriter on every one of those advertised films had probably started off with the same hopes for their film.

I am proud of *Jude*, and what I'm proudest of is that some people love the film passionately. That's certainly more than most films ever achieve. The difficulty has been in reconciling myself to the fact that it's not a film for everyone. I'd be lying if I said I didn't want to go away now and write a blockbuster that everyone liked, and everyone wanted to see. The bolder half of me wants to write challenging, provocative material but the frailer, more cautious side wants everyone to like it unreservedly. I hope there isn't a contradiction between the two, although my experience on *Jude* tells me that perhaps there is.

It was much easier and more pleasurable writing *Jude* than living with its release. I don't know whether it's because it's my first film, or because I'm oversensitive and neurotic, but I do know I haven't enjoyed the last few months like I should. Maybe I'll change, maybe I won't. I only hope I get a chance to make more films. Right now it's a great relief to be sitting at the word processor again, starting on a new script, thinking it's going to be the best one yet.

Hossein Amini,
October 1996

A Note on the Screenplay

The screenplay published here was the second draft copy that Andrew Eaton, Michael Winterbottom, and Mark Shivas took to Cannes to raise finance for the film. It was also the script that Polygram read when they decided to finance the film. It is several re-writes away from the final shooting script, but it is probably the draft that best reflects the writing before the requirements of the filmmaking took over. What appears here is an actual facsimile of the script as it existed at that moment, complete with typographical mistakes and other errors and omissions endemic to a working draft.

JUDE

SCREENPLAY BY HOSSEIN AMINI

Adapted from Thomas Hardy's
novel 'Jude the Obscure'

AT MARYGREEN

1. EXT. FARMER TROUTHAM'S FIELD. DAY.

A harrowed field stretches out before us, lost by degrees in the early morning mist.

A primal silence...

Suddenly we hear a loud clacking sound. The shadows of birds fill the mist. The beating of their wings shatters the silence...

The nine year old JUDE FAWLEY runs this way and that, spinning his clacker at the rooks as they try to feed. The birds take off in clusters, dark spots against the thick white mist...

JUDE stops to catch his breath. He watches the swirling flight of the birds above him. The rooks make faint patterns in the mist. JUDE stares thoughtfully. The clacker goes still in his hand...

The rooks glide away and settle in the distance...

JUDE watches the birds start to feed once again. He approaches them slowly this time. He throws the clacker away so they can be sure he's a friend...

JUDE steps closer and kneels down...

                    JUDE
          Go on then...Eat...Eat...

Suddenly the sound of the clacker starts up behind JUDE...

The birds take off in a frenzy...

A burly figure steps out of the mist and grabs JUDE by the scruff of the neck. FARMER TROUTHAM bends the boy over and smacks the clacker against his ass repeatedly...

                    FARMER TROUTHAM
          So you're giving them permission to eat are you...Eh?...My seed
          eh?...You've gone up in the world...

The rooks circle upwards and disappear into the swallowing mist...

The sound of the beating resounds across the field...

2. EXT. SCHOOLMASTER PHILLOTSON'S HOUSE. DAY.

A wooden crate slides heavily onto the back of the cart...

                    BLACKSMITH
          what do you keep in there?

                    PHILLOTSON
          It's all in the mind. Ready for some more?

The BLACKSMITH puffs heavily. SCHOOLMASTER PHILLOTSON slaps him on the back encouragingly and moves onto the next crate with good humor and boundless energy...

JUDE walks past the crowd with his head down. He enters his Aunt Drusilla's bake house...

1

3. INT. AUNT DRUSILLA'S BAKE HOUSE. DAY.

AUNT DRUSILLA knows it's JUDE without even looking around...

> AUNT DRUSILLA
> You've only been gone an hour.

AUNT DRUSILLA wipes the sweat and grease off her face and looks at JUDE...

She sees the tears in his eyes...

> AUNT DRUSILLA
> What's he done?

> JUDE
> Nothing.

> AUNT DRUSILLA
> He hit you?

The noise of the villagers packing and carting can be heard outside...

AUNT DRUSILLA glares at JUDE as she picks the bread off the grill with tough fingers...

> AUNT DRUSILLA
> Shame on you. His father was my father's journeyman...

4. EXT. SCHOOLMASTER PHILLOTSON'S HOUSE. DAY.

JUDE watches SCHOOLMASTER PHILLOTSON and his FRIENDS lift the last heavy box of books and walk it to the cart. JUDE still looks down from his beating that morning...

PHILLOTSON sees JUDE and calls out...

JUDE smiles back happily, honoured by his hero, his troubles forgotten...

He runs over and helps PHILLOTSON and his FRIENDS heave the heavy crate onto the cart...

5. EXT. ROAD OUT OF MARYGREEN. DAY.

The heavily laden cart moves along the black road...

JUDE follows at a discreet distance on foot...

PHILLOTSON pulls the reins and the horse comes to a stop. The schoolmaster is aware that JUDE is following him. He leans out of the cart and waves JUDE over with a friendly smile...

JUDE hesitates but then runs towards the cart excitedly...

6. INT. PHILLOTSON'S CART. DAY.

JUDE rides with PHILLOTSON. He keeps glancing at his hero shyly...

> PHILLOTSON
> Are you sorry I'm going Jude?

JUDE nods.

> PHILLOTSON
> So am I.

> JUDE
> Where are you going Sir?

> PHILLOTSON
> Christminster.

> JUDE
> Why do you have to go?

> PHILLOTSON
> You wouldn't understand Jude. You will perhaps when you're
> older.

> JUDE
> I think I would now Sir.

PHILLOTSON grins...

> PHILLOTSON
> You know what a University is, and a University degree?

JUDE shakes his head reluctantly, feeling stupid...

7. EXT. BROWN HOUSE BARN. DAY.

JUDE watches as PHILLOTSON climbs nimbly onto the barn roof. The sunset streaks the sky
above him...

8. EXT. BARN ROOF. DAY.

PHILLOTSON helps JUDE onto the roof...

JUDE looks down dizzily. The horse and cart are tied to the barn door...

PHILLOTSON walks to the edge of the barn roof and looks out as if over a magical kingdom...

JUDE watches his face. The schoolmaster is beaming with excitement as he takes in the
view...

> PHILLOTSON
> Come here Jude...

JUDE walks over cautiously...

The view suddenly opens up before him...

A huge spread of land reaches out into the distance and dissolves into the evening mist. A
blurred sunset blazes through the clouds...

> PHILLOTSON
> Do you see it? Over there...

3

PHILLOTSON points JUDE towards the limits of the stretch of landscape. Points of light shine through like topaz...

JUDE strains his eyes...

In the distance the mist has cleared a little. The points of topaz have turned into the faint outlines of domes and spires...

                    PHILLOTSON
        That's Christminster...

The schoolmaster stares at the city in reverent awe. His eyes are full of dreams...

                    PHILLOTSON
        If you want to do anything in life Jude that's where you have
        to go. Even if it means giving up everything else for a while...

The sunlight begins to glimmer throught the clouds...

                    PHILLOTSON
        You have to read your books when your friends are out
        playing. Get out of bed early in the morning when it's freezing
        cold. Study every chance you get. One day it will all pay off I
        promise you...

The vanes and windows and wet roof slates of the city glint in the light...

                    PHILLOTSON
        Once you're there everything's open to you. You can become
        anything you want. You can choose your future.

The sun breaks through the clouds. The city changes shap before their eyes...

9. INT. TEN YEARS LATER/ VILLAGE CHURCH. DAY.

JUDE clambers down the Church scaffolding...

Down below the other STONEMASONS are lying on squares of white canvas, eating their lunch. There's stone dust everywhere. The whole Church is covered in sack cloth...

JUDE walks towards the exit in a hurry...

The other STONEMASONS rib him on his way:

                  1ST STONEMASON
        What's wrong with us Jude?

                  2ND STONEMASON
        Who've you got waiting?

JUDE grins mysteriously and walks out...

10. EXT. WOODLAND PATH. DAY.

The sunlight pours through the trees. There's the sound of a rushing stream in the distance...

JUDE walks along the woodland path with his sack on his back. He turns around to make sure no-one's following him and heads off into the woods...

11. EXT. WOODLAND. DAY.

The sound of the rushing stream is louder here. JUDE makes himself comfortable on the rough earth. He reaches into his sack and pulls out a leather bound book. He opens it reverently. The type script is in Greek...

JUDE starts to read falteringly...

                    JUDE
He handed over the wondrous Briseis to the Greeks...to take away...Then the great Achilles left his companions, far away....and sat on the sand and stared out at the sea...

12. EXT. TREES. DAY.

We hear the tread of feet through the trees. Branches being quietly swept aside. Whispering...

13. EXT. WOODLAND. DAY.

JUDE is completely absorbed in his book. He mouths the words. He struggles over certain lines but wills himself on...

                    JUDE
"Mother you gave me life...however short that life...and promised me honour...Yet now Agammemnon shames me and takes my prize..."

There's a sound of cracking branches nearby. JUDE is too absorbed to notice. His face is knotted in concentration. His reading seems more like a battle than a pleasure...

                    JUDE
And so he wept and cursed and prayed...And his mother heard him and rose from the sea like a mist..."My son, why do you weep?"

Suddenly something flies through the air and smacks JUDE on the ear...

He recoils sharply, wiping his face as if he's been stung...

14. EXT. TREES. DAY.

There's a rush of feet through the trees. We hear muffled giggling as the unseen perpetrators run away...

15. EXT. WOODLAND. DAY.

JUDE picks up what it was that hit him. The red wet flesh slips through his hand. It's a pig's penis...

JUDE looks around the woodland. He sees nothing but the glinting of the sun through the trees. He listens carefully. There's laughter in the distance...

16. EXT. STREAM. DAY.

Three young GIRLS kneel by the brook with buckets at their feet. They appear to be washing clothes in the river...

JUDE stares at them from across the stream. They don't notice him or pretend not to...

The girls' buckets are full of pigs' innards. They scoop up handfuls of pink flesh and let the river wash the blood away...

One of the GIRLS glances at JUDE. She can't hide a sly smile. The others try to stop themselves giggling...

JUDE is now sure it was them...

JUDE
Thank you very much.

One of the GIRLS turns to her neighbour innocently:

1ST GIRL

I didn't throw it.

2ND GIRL
Nor me.

3rd GIRL
Anny how could you?

1ST GIRL
I didn't throw it. I don't even like the look of him.

The three of them carry on with their work as if JUDE wasn't there...

JUDE
So none of you threw it?

One of the GIRLS stands up casually and looks across at JUDE. She's a voluptuous looking girl. The sweat shines off her skin.

3RD GIRL (ARABELLA)
I'll tell you what. You come over here and I'll whisper who it
was in your ear.

The other girls giggle...

JUDE looks embarrassed. He doesn't know how to reply...

6

                    ARABELLA
        Alright then, I'll come to you.

ARABELLA stares at him for a moment and then walks towards a small plank bridge that
leads across the stream...

17. EXT. PLANK BRIDGE. DAY.

                    ARABELLA
        I bet you think I threw it?

                    JUDE
        No.

                    ARABELLA
        Well I did, but don't tell anyone.

                    JUDE
        I can't tell anyone. I don't even know your name.

                    ARABELLA
        Shall I tell it to you?

                    JUDE
        If you like.

                    ARABELLA
        Arabella Donn.

JUDE can't help staring into her eyes...

                    ARABELLA
        My father's the pig breeder. Those are my friends. We were
        washing innards for black pudding.

JUDE looks from her eyes to her mouth and tries to stop himself looking at her ample
bosom...

                    ARABELLA
        What?

                    JUDE
        Nothing. You're a nice looking girl.

                    ARABELLA
        You should see me on Sundays.

                    JUDE
        I'd like to.

He says it hesitantly. ARABELLA takes her time...

                    ARABELLA
        That's alright. No-one's after me just now.

7

She stares into his eyes coolly...

> JUDE
> Tomorrow's Sunday?

> ARABELLA
> That's right.

JUDE can't think of anything else to say. ARABELLA shrugs, smiles goodbye, and walks back across the bridge with all the confidence in the world...

JUDE watches her. He looks irritated with himself...

18. EXT. STREAM. DAY.

ARABELLA is the only one of the girls who doesn't watch JUDE disappear back into the woods. She's playing hard to get. It's only when he's gone that she looks up from her work...

> ANNY
> I think you've caught one there.

ARABELLA stares at the spot of woodland where JUDE disappeared. She doesn't look convinced...

> ARABELLA
> I should have thrown something else at him.

19. INT. AUNT DRUSILLA'S HOUSE. NIGHT.

AUNT DRUSILLA and JUDE sit by the fire. The old woman has a blanket over her legs. She's reading a letter. She passes a photograph from the same envelope for JUDE to have a look at...

> AUNT DRUSILLA
> I don't know why she bothers to send a picture of herself.
> She's looking far too prim and thin...

JUDE has a look...

It's a grainy photograph of a beautiful young girl...

JUDE is immediately struck by her looks...

> JUDE
> She looks alright to me.

> AUNT DRUSILLA
> Who doesn't.

JUDE smiles. He keeps looking at the girl in the picture...

> AUNT DRUSILLA
> She's lost her smile the silly girl. All city airs and graces.

8

                    JUDE
What's she doing in Christminster?

                    AUNT DRUSILLA
She doesn't day.

                    JUDE
I'll have to visit her.

                    AUNT DRUSILLA
You won't like her.

JUDE smiles at AUNT DRUSILLA's crustiness. He teases her gently...

                    JUDE
I'm sure I will Aunt. We're family.

                    AUNT DRUSILLA
Well she certainly won't like you.

                    JUDE
Why not?

                    AUNT DRUSILLA
She's far to clever and townish for you. She'll look right down
her nose at a thick country boy.

JUDE laughs...

                    JUDE
You seem very fond of her.

                    AUNT DRUSILLA
And you seem interested in everything but your books tonight
Jude.

JUDE grins and looks at the photograph of his cousin Sue again...

20. INT. JUDE'S BEDROOM. DAWN.

                    JUDE
...Proffessing themselves to be wise they became fools, and
changed the glory of the incorruptible God into an image made
like to corruptible man and to birds, and four footed beasts
and creeping things...

JUDE is hunched over his Latin New Testament. He's finding it hard to concentrate...

He gets up and walks to the window...

Outside the sun is beginning to light the morning. Trees float in the mist...

JUDE stares back into the dark room guiltily, knowing he should get back to his reading...

Instead he looks out of the window again...

21. EXT. PATH LEADING TO ARABELLA'S HOUSE. DAY.

JUDE is wearing his Sunday best. He walks briskly, excitedly...

22. EXT. ARABELLA'S HOUSE. DAY.

There's a loud snorting of pigs coming from behind the house...

JUDE stares at the ground separating him from Arabella's house. It's wet and thick with pig shit...

JUDE tugs his trouser legs up and cakes his Sunday shoes in filth as he treks across the swill...

From inside the house JUDE hears a rough VOICE calling out:

> FATHER'S VOICE OFFSCREEN
> Arabella! Hurry up! Your young man's here!

A moment later ARABELLA opens the front door. She looks embarrassed...

> ARABELLA
> I'd rather go out, wouldn't you?

23. EXT. THE GREAT DOWN. DAY.

ARABELLA follows JUDE up the steep ascent. He keeps looking at her to make sure she's alright. She pulls exhausted faces and makes him laugh...

ARABELLA collapses at the top of the slope. She stretches out her arms akimbo and shuts her eyes dramatically. She's playing dead...

> ARABELLA
> Even if you kissed me you couldn't bring me back to life.

> JUDE
> What if I tickled you?

> ARABELLA
> You wouldn't dare.

JUDE laughs again. But she's right. He's too shy to touch her...

24. EXT. WOODLAND. DAY.

ARABELLA looks around Jude's hideaway in the woods...

> ARABELLA
> And all you do here is read?

> JUDE
> Yes.

> ARABELLA
> Nothing else?

She looks at him slyly.

JUDE doesn't understand...

> ARABELLA
> What do you read?

> JUDE
> Latin. Some Greek. I've read two books of the Illiad.
> Thuciydes. Heciod. Some of the Greek Testament...

> ARABELLA
> My, my.

> JUDE
> Well I need to if I'm going to get into Christminster.

> ARABELLA
> Christminster.

> JUDE
> Yes. I'm going to be a scholar, and then maybe even a
> professor one day.

> ARABELLA
> Well Hoity Toity...

It takes JUDE a moment to realise she's teasing him...

ARABELLA grins mischievously...

JUDE laughs at himself...

> ARABELLA
> Have you ever seen me climb a tree?

> JUDE
> No.

JUDE looks confused by the random change of topic...

ARABELLA takes off her shoes and gives them to JUDE...

She strides towards the nearest tree and starts to climb it like a monkey...

JUDE watches her in disbelief...

> JUDE
> You're mad...

ARABELLA's skirt rides up her long tanned legs...

She laughs at him as she climbs...

She stretches her leg from one branch to another, completely uninhibited...

JUDE gets a glimpse up her skirt...

He looks down in embarrassment...

                              ARABELLA
          Jude?... Jude?!

JUDE looks up hesitantly. ARABELLA is high up in the tree...

JUDE can't help but be charmed by her childish excitement and unpredictability...

25. EXT. PATH DOWN TO ARABELLA'S HOUSE. NIGHT.

ARABELLA and JUDE walk close together. They're almost touching.

ARABELLA suddenly stops as she sees the lights of her house appear at the foot of the hill.
She seems reluctant to continue...
                              JUDE
          What is it?

ARABELLA stares at her house as if it's a prison she's returning to...
                              ARABELLA
          Put your arm around me Jude. Just for a moment.

There's a touching frailty in her voice...

JUDE puts his arm around her...

26. EXT. LOOKING THROUGH THE WINDOW OF ARABELLA'S HOUSE. NIGHT.

Through the frosted pane we see ARABELLA'S PARENTS drinking noisily with their
NEIGHBOURS.

ARABELLA hesitates at the door.

                              JUDE
          We can keep walking if you like. It's not late.

ARABELLA looks at JUDE gratefully...

27. EXT. PIGSTY. NIGHT.

The sound of the pigs squelching and snorting in their sty is deafening. JUDE sees the
vague shapes of animals moving in the darkness. From a distance the pigs look like a
sinister fluid mass...

ARABELLA hurries JUDE into the barn before he's put off by the swine...

28. INT. PIG BREEDER'S BARN/ LOWER LEVEL. NIGHT.

It's dark in the barn. ARABELLA squats in the hay. She looks ungraceful with her knees up to
her face, but somehow sexy...

                              JUDE
          Get up Abby.

                    ARABELLA
     Why?

                    JUDE
     I want to kiss you.

                    ARABELLA
     Kiss me like this.

JUDE walks towards her hesitantly...

ARABELLA breathes gently in the dark...

JUDE stares at her thick thighs and her breasts...

ARABELLA covers her cleavage with her hands. Her voice is almost a whisper...

                    ARABELLA
     Be careful. I am part eggshell.

JUDE looks confused. He doesn't understand what she means...

ARABELLA slowly unfastens the collar of her gown. From between her breasts she produces
a small egg wrapped in wool...

                    ARABELLA
     I am hatching an egg. I will carry it with me everywhere. It will
     hatch in three days.

ARABELLA slips the egg back between her breasts...

JUDE's voice in unsteady...

                    JUDE
     Why do you do such a strange thing?

                    ARABELLA
     It's not strange. It's natural for a woman to bring a live thing
     into the world.

JUDE can't help staring at her cleavage...

                    ARABELLA
     You mustn't touch me now... You should have caught me a
     minute ago when I took the egg out...

JUDE can't speak...

ARABELLA dips her fingers down her front and takes the egg out again...

JUDE kneels down beside her...

ARABELLA stares into his eyes and slips the egg back down her front...

This time Jude's fingers follow. She doesn't stop him. He takes the egg from between her
breasts and kisses her open neck...

                         13

ARABELLA leans back onto the hay, pulling him down with her...

29. INT. AUNT DRUSILLA'S HOUSE. NIGHT.

JUDE walks quietly past Aunt Drusilla's bedroom...

She's left her door open...

Just as JUDE thinks he's safe, she calls out of the dark...

> AUNT DRUSILLA OFFSCREEN
> Jude?

> JUDE
> Yes.

> AUNT DRUSILLA OFFSCREEN
> It's late.

Mercifully that's all she asks. JUDE continues quietly towards his bedroom...

30. INT. JUDE'S BEDROOM. NIGHT.

JUDE walks into his bedroom as if he's late for an appointment. He gropes his way through the dark until he finds the gas lamp. He lights it...

The Greek book is still on the desk, open at the same page he left it...

JUDE sits down guiltily and forces himself to read...

31. EXT. VIEW OF CHRISTMINSTER. DAWN.

Christminster floats in the dawn mist like a shapeless phantom...

32. EXT. STREAM. DAY.

JUDE stares at the rushing stream...

ARABELLA touches his shoulder gently...

> ARABELLA
> What's wrong?

> JUDE
> Nothing.

> ARABELLA
> You've been like this all day.

> JUDE
> It's got nothing to do with you. I'm angry with myself.

> ARABELLA
> Why?

14

JUDE
Because I'm not reading enough. I'm not studying enough.

ARABELLA
Maybe you don't want to.

JUDE
Of course I do. Bella you've only known me a few weeks. All
I've ever dreamt about is educating myself enough to get to
University.

ARABELLA
And then what?

JUDE
Anything. Anything will be possible...

ARABELLA
But I can give you everything you want.

JUDE
Arabella...

ARABELLA
Maybe you've changed.

JUDE
No.

JUDE hesitates. He doesn't know quite how to tell her. He tries to sound matter of fact...

JUDE
I think the thing to do is just go there...

ARABELLA
To Christminster?

JUDE
Yes. If I'm there I'll have to study.

ARABELLA tries to keep her voice steady...

ARABELLA
What about me?

JUDE
I think I ought to go... now, whilst it's not too late for both of
us...

Tears fill ARABELLA's eyes but her voice is calm and dignified...

ARABELLA
How do you know it's not too late?

JUDE turns and looks at her for the first time. Her bloodshot eyes burn into him. He
doesn't understand...

15

                              ARABELLA
                    I didn't want to tell you like this...

JUDE stares in confusion...

                              ARABELLA
                    I'm pregnant Jude.

JUDE smiles tightly and looks away. He can't speak. He finds it hard to look at ARABELLA...

He tries to force a smile, but it's too weak to be convincing. JUDE can't hide his feelings.
He's filled with a quiet suffocating panic...

ARABELLA refuses to make it easy for him. She won't speak until he does. She just stares at
him expectantly...

JUDE struggles with himself. He knows he has to be strong for Arabella. He finally looks up
at her...

This time his smile is a little more convincing...

33. EXT. ARABELLA'S HOUSE/ FIELD/ WEDDING. DAY.

ARABELLA is dressed in her white wedding dress, with a beautiful garland of flowers in her
hair. She squats on the floor, surrounded by excitable LITTLE BRIDESMAIDS...

ARABELLA is showing the BRIDESMAIDS her favourite wedding present. It's a cute little pig
with a black spot on its head. ARABELLA tickles its belly...

                              ARABELLA
                    What shall we call her? You all get to choose a name.

                            1ST BRIDESMAID
          Rosie.

                              ARABELLA
          Not bad. Not bad. Any more?

                            2ND BRIDESMAID
          Jemima Spot.

ARABELLA laughs...

JUDE watches her from the groom's table...

33A. EXT. FIELD/ WEDDING LATER. DAY.

The LITTLE BRIDESMAIDS are playing a game of touch the pig and run away...

They surround the animal, giggling and shrieking in mock terror...

They take turns to run up to it and pull its tail...

ARABELLA laughs as the little girls run and scream happily...

16

She's sitting on JUDE's lap, taking spoonfuls of leftover wedding cake off his plate...

> JUDE
> Are you still hungry?

> ARABELLA
> It's for you.

She gives JUDE a deep kiss with crumbs and cream still in her mouth...

34. INT. JUDE'S HOUSE. NIGHT.

The bedside lamp casts the room in glowing patterns. JUDE lies in bed, watching ARABELLA slowly undress...

She moves in and out of the shadows, folding her discarded clothes, teasing him...

JUDE sits up to get a better look...

ARABELLA turns her back on him and unfastens her bunched up hair. It falls in a cascade across her naked skin...

JUDE stares at her...

ARABELLA smiles at him invitingly. She puts her hands behind her neck and tugs loose her tail of hair. It comes off easily in her hands...

JUDE looks surprised...

> JUDE
> It isn't all your own...?

> ARABELLA
> So?

She turns away casually and hangs her hair extension on a mirror. When she turns around JUDE is still staring...

> ARABELLA
> What?

> JUDE
> You've enough of your own hair, surely.

> ARABELLA
> It's fashionable in the big cities.

> JUDE
> What do you care what people think in the big cities?

> ARABELLA
> Don't you like it?

> JUDE
> No.

17

ARABELLA
Then I won't wear it.

JUDE feels bad for being irritable. He looks apologetic...

ARABELLA cheers up easily. The seductive smile comes back and she perches at the end of the bed...

JUDE is about to turn the gas lamp off...

ARABELLA
...Leave it on... I want to see us...

JUDE looks surprised and a little embarrassed...

With a mischievous smile ARABELLA pulls the sheets away slowly...

ARABELLA
You can close your eyes if you like and pretend it's dark...

ARABELLA lets the sheets fall onto the floor...

She crawls towards JUDE on all fours until she straddles his chest...

JUDE stares up at her...

ARABELLA
Your mouth looks dry...

ARABELLA swills some saliva in her mouth and suddenly bends down and kisses him...

JUDE responds at once...

Just as his arms reach out to grab her ARABELLA pulls her mouth away...

JUDE hesitates...

She smiles at him mischievously...

ARABELLA
Ask me nicely...

JUDE doesn't understand...

JUDE
Ask you what?

ARABELLA
Whatever you want me to do...

Her openness makes JUDE uncomfortable...

JUDE
I don't know...

                    ARABELLA
        Then I'll have to make it up...

ARABELLA leans down and blows over his nipples...

35. EXT. FIELD OUTSIDE JUDE'S HOUSE. DAY.

The sound of an icy wind...

The field and the trees beyond it are completely covered in snow...

Suddenly the squealing of a pig shrills through the winter silence...

36. INT. JUDE'S HOUSE. DAY.

JUDE feeds bean stalks into the fire. Water boils in a copper pot...

The sound of the pig's squealing can still be heard outside...

ARABELLA moves Jude's books from the table to clear a space...

                    JUDE
        Arabella...

                    ARABELLA
        What?

                    JUDE
        Be careful with those.

                    ARABELLA
        Then find somewhere else for them. This table is for the lard.

She sounds confrontational...

37. EXT. OUTSIDE THE STY/ JUDE'S HOUSE. DAY.

The pig screams...

ARABELLA loops its legs with a cord...

It's the same pig with the black spot on its head, except older, fatter, and ready for slaughter...

The pig struggles desperately in the snow. ARABELLA tightens the cord until the animal is exhausted. Its cry turns from rage to despair...

ARABELLA steps back, pleased with her handiwork...

JUDE looks at the pig with pity...

                    ARABELLA
        There's the sticking knife. Whatever you do, don't cut him too
        deep.

                    JUDE
I'll just make it quick.

                    ARABELLA
You can't. The meat has to bleed slowly. Just touch the vein.

                    JUDE
No.

                    ARABELLA
I was brought up doing this. I know. He has to die slowly.
Eight or ten minutes at least...

JUDE plunges the knife as deeply as he can into the pig's neck...

ARABELLA lets out a cry of frustration...

                    ARABELLA
        Damn it!

The blood flows out in a torrent, spreading through the snow...

The pig chokes and gurgles liquid...

                    ARABELLA
You overstuck it. I told you!

JUDE stares at the dying animal, paralysed...

ARABELLA snatches the knife off him angrily, falls to her knees on the snow, digs the blade
into the pig's bubbling wound, and slits its windpipe expertly...

The pig is instantly silent, its dying breath coming through the hole...

JUDE keeps staring at the carcass and the bloodspatter spreading far out into the snow...

                    ARABELLA
There. You've lost all the blood. I can't make any blackpot
now.

JUDE looks sickened. His voice is barely audible...

                    JUDE
Thank God it's dead.

                    ARABELLA
What's God got to do with pig killing!

ARABELLA turns away from him scornfully and starts scooping handfuls of bloody snow into
her pail...

JUDE opens a book...

He wipes some grease off the pages irritably...

He tries to read...

Outside there's a sickening noise of chopping...

JUDE can't concentrate...

He turns towards the window...

37B. EXT. JUDE'S POV / OUTSIDE THE HOUSE. DAY.

ARABELLA turns the pigs carcass over...

She catches her breath...

Her arms are covered in blood...

She bends down and starts scraping away some skin with her knife. She digs into the pigs open belly with her hands...

38. EXT. JUDE'S HOUSE. DAY.

JUDE storms out of the house. He doesn't bother to shut the door...

It creaks in the wind behind him...

ARABELLA doesn't even look up...

39. EXT. ROAD TO AUNT DRUSILLA'S HOUSE. DAY.

JUDE looks angry...

He kicks at the snow...

He suddenly walks off the path and onto the ice...

We see him walk across the frozen lake...

In the distance we see him skidding and sliding like a kid...

40. INT. AUNT DRUSILLA'S HOUSE. NIGHT.

The photograph of Sue has been framed. It sits on the mantlepiece between two brass candlesticks...

JUDE stares at the picture...

AUNT DRUSILLA watches him from the fireplace...

> AUNT DRUSILLA
> Haven't you had enough of women for one night?

JUDE smiles sadly...

> AUNT DRUSILLA
> I won't feel sorry for you. You should have listened to me.
> Fawleys are not cut out for marriage.

> JUDE
> I had no choice.

> AUNT DRUSILLA
> You had no brains. She's five months pregnant and not even a
> bulge.

> JUDE
> Please don't say that Aunt.

He sounds upset.

> AUNT DRUSILLA
> I'll get your old bedroom ready.

> JUDE
> No I'd better go...

JUDE turns away from the picture of Sue...

40A. EXT. JUDE'S HOUSE. NIGHT.

The door is still open as Jude left it...

It creaks in the wind...

41. INT. JUDE'S HOUSE. NIGHT.

JUDE walks into his house...

The room is covered in grease and fat and scallops. What's left of the pig's carcass lies at
the foot of the table...

There is no sign of Arabella...

A letter is pinned to the cotton blower by the fireplace...

As JUDE approaches, we hear ARABELLA'S VOICEOVER FADE UP...

> ARABELLA VOICEOVER
> I've gone back to my family Jude and I won't be back. These
> last few weeks I've grown as tired of you as you have of me. I
> don't care for the sort of life you lead and I can't see it
> changing. As for the child, don't worry, it looks like I made a
> mistake. You may find this hard to believe but I did not set out
> to deceive you. I swear I thought it was true...

JUDE stares at the letter...

22

ARABELLA VOICEOVER (cont)
Perhaps now you will be free to read your books and go where you've always wanted to go. I hope you have no objection to my leaving...

The sound of the wind on the windows turns into the speeding wheels of a train...

41A. EX. RAILWAY TRACKS, DAY.

Tracks opening and tightening below us in patterns...

Pebbles spitting up at us...

AT CHRISTMINSTER

42. INT. RELIGIOUS STATIONERY SHOP. DAY.

A pair of delicate hands scratch a sharp tool across a piece of zinc. The letters stand out as if illuminated...

SUE BRIDESHEAD is bent over her desk, concentrating on her work...

JUDE watches her out of the corner of his eye. She looks even more beautiful than her photograph...

JUDE pretends he's browsing through the shop. His eyes keep drifting from the stacked shelves and the religious knick knacks to Sue's desk...

SUE gets up and walks over to the shop counter...

JUDE stares hard at a plaster angel on the shelf. He's trying to listen to Sue's voice as she talks to the two ELDERLY WOMEN at the front desk. All JUDE can hear is her whisper...

JUDE glimpses round as SUE walks back to her desk. Their eyes meet for an instant. SUE smiles politely.

JUDE looks flustered. He picks up the plaster angel. He has to buy it now...

43. EXT. RELIGIOUS STATIONERY SHOP. DAY.

SUE walks out of the shop and heads down the street...

JUDE watches her...

44. EXT. COLLEGE LANE. DAY.

JUDE follows SUE into one of the college lanes. He keeps a discreet distance...

A group of STUDENTS IN BLACK GOWNS walk out of their college gate. They all glance at SUE in admiration. She ignores them and carries on walking...

JUDE smiles at the STUDENTS as they walk past...

Not one of them acknowledges him...

45. EXT. HIGH STREET/ CHRISTMINSTER. DAY.

The sunlight glints on the gothic towers of Christminster...

Down below there's a deafening noise of people. The streets are stained with rotten fruit and vegetables from the morning's market...

JUDE finds himself walking against the flow, trying to look over people's heads and shoulders to find Sue...

He catches sight of her briefly and then loses here in the crowd...

46. INT. JUDE'S LODGINGS/ CHRISTMINSTER. NIGHT.

The framed picture of Sue sits on the window sill...

JUDE places the plaster Angel next to it...

The spires of Christminster are lit up like beacons...

JUDE translates his Greek aloud...

> JUDE
> ...Through me tell the story of Odysseus the wanderer... harried by the Gods... exiled by the Gods... after he plundered the castle of Troy...

47. EXT. SUE'S LODGINGS/ CHRISTMINSTER. DAY.

SUE leaves her lodgings...

A light mist covers the narrow lane...

Her footsteps echo on the cobbled streets as she turns the corner...

JUDE's been waiting all the time. He follows her unseen...

47A. EXT. CHIEF STREET. DAY.

SUE runs across the busy street despite the oncoming omnibus...

It's almost as if she knows someone is following her...

JUDE is left on the pavement...

He watches her dart nimbly through the traffic...

JUDE sets off after her...

He narrowly avoids a speeding horse and carriage...

48. INT. PUBLIC HALL / CHRISTMINSTER. DAY.

A CROWD OF LABOURERS are gathered in a dreary hall...

A heavily bearded DEMAGOGUE harangues the CROWD from a makeshift stage...

> DEMAGOGUE
> ...There are two Christminsters. There's your dreaming spires and scholars and then there's your back to back houses, and your grubby children hanging off scaffolding lost their way to school...

The speakers' ASSISTANTS hand out leaflets...

> DEMAGOGUE (Cont)
> It's the same city. Maybe a five minute walk from Church street to scum street. Why don't we go over? Why don't we

go over and knock on their doors? Because they've convinced us this is the way it is. No change. Why change?

JUDE spots SUE in the crowd. She's the only woman there. She's pushing her way steadily to the front...

                    DEMAGOGUE (Cont)
          They've won their argument. They educate their kind to win
          that argument. What do you do? You give your eight year old
          a pat on the back because he's left school to get a job? So he
          ends up happy just like you. Living with his Auntie, and his
          Auntie's Auntie, and her kids. Life's good. Ten square foots a
          palace.

There are a few laughs...

                    DEMAGOGUE (Cont)
          Don't laugh because it's not funny. Poor people laugh at
          themselves. And Rich people laugh at them too. The joke's on
          you...

49. EXT STONEYARD/ CHRISTMINSTER. DAY.

An oven spits and sparks as the STONEMASONS take turns to fire-sharpen their tools...

There's a deafening noise of cracking stones. The MASONS kneel all around the stoneyard walls, hand sawing monumental blocks. A veil of thin white dust hangs over the courtyard...

JUDE digs a claw tool through a piece of granite. His shirt is soaked with sweat. He looks up as he takes a brief rest...

Through the mist of white dusk JUDE sees a WOMAN walking into the stoneyard. JUDE can't believe his eyes. It looks like Sue...

The WOMAN approaches the FOREMAN and talks to him...

JUDE can't hear a word through the hammering of stone. He stares nervously...

Suddenly the FOREMAN points in Jude's direction. The WOMAN approaches. JUDE drops his tools in panic and stands up, wiping his hands on his overalls...

SUE approaches through the white dust like a vision. She smiles at JUDE warmly:

                    SUE
          Jude Fawley?

JUDE nods...

                    SUE
          I'm your cousin, Sue Bridehead.

JUDE smiles a greeting. He can't think of anything to say.

                              SUE
        Aunt Drusilla wrote and told me you were here in
        Christminster...

She stops. The noise of cracking stone drowns her out...

                              SUE
        I can't hear myself speak...

SCENE 50 CUT

51. EXT. COURTYARD TAVERN. DAY.

The courtyard is set with long tables and benches. Everyone sits together. ARTISANS and
TRADESMEN drink and chat noisily...

SUE and JUDE sit with some half drunk STONEMASONS...

                           UNCLE JOE
        ...Don't either of you take this wrong but you don't look like
        cousins to me.

                              SUE
        Why is that Uncle Joe?

                           UNCLE JOE
        Because you're pretty and fine and Jude here looks like a great
        big mallet's squashed his face...

The other STONEMASONS laugh...

                          TINKER TAYLOR
        A flat face is a sign of nobility, it's a sign of nobility...

No-one pays any attention to TINKER TAYLOR...

                           UNCLE JIM
        May I just point out that they have the same nose.

                           UNCLE JOE
        Rubbish.

                           UNCLE JIM
        Rubbish yourself. Look at them. Smooth hillocks, gentle
        climbing slopes, you can almost see the deer running up
        them...

There's laughter around the table...

JUDE grins nervously. He's worried that SUE won't like his friends...

SUE's completely at ease with the MEN...

                              SUE
        Tell me some more about my cousin...

                              27

TINKER TAYLOR
                    He's a scholar, a true scholar...

No-one listens to TINKER TAYLOR...

                            UNCLE JOE
                    He's a sinner.

                            SUE
                    And why's that?

                            UNCLE JOE
                    What was the last one called Jim?

                            UNCLE JIM
                    You mean Vicky.

                            UNCLE JOE
                    No Florence.

                            UNCLE JIM
                    The one before Elsbeth.

There's more laughter at JUDE's expense...

SUE laughs loudest of all...

52. EXT. CHRISTMINSTER STREET. DAY.

SUE is still laughing and ribbing JUDE as they walk down the cobbled street...

                            SUE
                    Why should I believe you and not them?

                            JUDE
                    Because it's obvious I'm not that sort of person.

                            SUE
                    How do I know that?

                            JUDE
                    You must be able to tell.

                            SUE
                    How can I? I've only just met you.

                            JUDE
                    Well, I've only just met you and I feel like I've known you all my
                    life.

SUE smiles. She's touched by his sweetness...

                            SUE
                    Well you haven't. You don't know anything about me yet.

JUDE and SUE stand outside the cold grey building...

> JUDE
> So who lives here?

> SUE
> Just me and an old lady with red teeth and claws.

> JUDE
> You're mad.

> SUE
> It runs in the family.

JUDE stares at her for a moment...

SUE sticks out her hand...

> SUE
> Nice to meet you Jude.

JUDE shakes hands...

He's a little taken aback by the formality...

> JUDE
> I'm free all day tomorrow.

> SUE
> I'm not.

There's a knock on the window above them...

JUDE looks up.

The grim looking LANDLADY stares down disapprovingly...

54. EXT. STONEYARD. DAY.

The MASONS are cracking stones...

UNCLE JIM and UNCLE JOE tease JUDE as they work...

> UNCLE JOE
> What does the law say about marrying your cousin?

> UNCLE JIM
> I don't know about that, but it says nothing about falling in
> love with them.

> UNCLE JOE
> Is that so?

29

                         UNCLE JIM
           It's quite common I hear.

JUDE smiles and ignores them. He keeps breaking stones...

                         UNCLE JOE
           What do you think Jude?

                         JUDE
           You two are cousins. You tell me.

TINKER TAYLOR laughs...

55. EXT. HIGH STREET/ CHRISTMINSTER. DAY.

JUDE paces anxiously...

                         SUE OFFSCREEN
           Jude!

JUDE looks around. SUE stands across the road from him...

                         SUE
           Not there. It's bad luck.

JUDE looks down at his feet. There's a cross embedded in the pavement.

                         SUE
           They used to burn martyrs there.

JUDE steps off the cross and walks towards her...

SUE greets him with an easy smile...

                         SUE
           Are you superstitious Jude?

                         JUDE
           No.

                         SUE
           Nor am I. But I think it's best to be safe don't you think?

SUE laughs at herself. JUDE smiles.

                         JUDE
           I thought we could go to...

                         SUE
           No no no I'm taking you somewhere tonight.

She takes his hand and pulls him along before he has a chance to say anything...

SUE pulls JUDE along an old stone street surrounded by looming college walls and turrets...

                    JUDE
          Where?

                    SUE
          Somewhere living. Away from all this gloom.

                    JUDE
          But it's wonderful here.

                    SUE
          It's all stone.

                    JUDE
          You're talking about the buildings. I'm talking about the
          scholars.

                    SUE
          I was talking about the scholars too.

57. EXT. LIVESTOCK MARKET/ CHRISTMINSTER. DUSK.

A deafening noise of barter...

Livestock kick and pull as they're presented for purchase...

Chickens and rabbits are crammed into wire cages. The stink and din is oppressive...

                    JUDE
          So this is the real Christminster?

                    SUE
          No but this is where all our ideas will come from, not your
          musty libraries.

                    JUDE
          You're too modern for me.

SUE grins and heads for some gypsy stalls in the distance...

JUDE follows happily...

58. EXT. GYPSY STALL. DUSK.

The GYPSY SALESMAN sits by his wares. An oil lamp flickers over his statuettes. They're pagan figures, Greek Gods and Goddesses in half obscene poses...

SUE looks nervously at the objects...

The GYPSY SALESMAN says nothing. He waits patiently for SUE to get over her embarrassment...

                              JUDE
              You're not really going to buy them?

                              SUE
              How much are these two please?

SUE half gestures towards a statue of Cupid and one of Apollo...

                      GYPSY SALESMAN
              Ten Shillings.

SUE hesitates.

JUDE can't believe she'll go through with it...

                      GYPSY SALESMAN
              Would you like me to wrap them up?

                              SUE
              No thank you.

59. EXT. MARKET/ BEERSHEBA. DUSK.

JUDE picks up vegetables leaves from the pavement. SUE wraps her statuettes in the
greenery as well as she can. They look like giant misshapen cabbages. JUDE puts on a high
pitched landlady's voice and teases her gently...

                              JUDE
              That's a strange looking vegetable you're bought yourself Miss
              Bridehead...

60. INT. PUB. DUSK.

JUDE and SUE sit opposite each other in the dimly lit tavern...

The green wrapped statuettes are on the table between them...

                              SUE
              They're nicer to look at than any Church statues.

                              JUDE
              They why have you wrapped them up?

                              SUE
              Because I don't want to give my landlady an unnecessary heart
              attack. You're being rather confrontational.

                              JUDE
              No I was just wondering why you bother to go to Church at all?

                              SUE
              Because a part of me is still a superstitious backward country
              girl.

                              JUDE
              You mean like me?

                              32

                    SUE
          I didn't know you were a girl.

JUDE shrugs as if to say it's no use arguing with her...

                    SUE
          Do I irritate you?

                    JUDE
          No.

                    SUE
          Even when I keep trying to prove how much cleverer than you
          I am.

                    JUDE
          You are.

                    SUE
          Don't say that.

                    JUDE
          Why not?

                    SUE
          Because it's not the sort of thing you should admit to.

                    JUDE
          Why not? If it's true?

This time SUE has no answer...

They stare at each other...

                    SUE
          Say something.

                    JUDE
          I enjoy listening to you.

                    SUE
          what's that in your jacket pocket?

                    JUDE
          Nothing.

                    SUE
          It can't be nothing. I've been looking at it all day.

JUDE takes the book out of his pocket and hands it to SUE...

                    SUE
          I see. Catullus...

SUE gives him a mischievous smile and a raised eyebrow...

JUDE blushes...

SUE holds the book upside down and lets it open at the most thumbed page...

She translates the Latin...

> SUE
> Godlike the man who sits at her side, who watches and catches
> the laughter which softly tears me to tatters: nothing is left of
> me each time I see her...

SUE stops and looks up at JUDE...

> SUE
> It's beautiful.

JUDE looks proud, almost as if he'd written the poem himself...

> SUE
> Shall I read you my favourite Catullus?

JUDE smiles yes...

SUE flicks through the pages until she finds the poem...

She clears her throat and looks at him meaningfully...

> SUE
> Formianuses whore, long nosed, well stuffed Ameana, claims
> that I owe her a thousand, for services. Gather round friends
> and relations call in your medical practitioners. She is clearly
> mad...

JUDE laughs and snatches the book off her...

SCENE 61 CUT

62. EXT. BIBLIOL COLLEGE QUADRANGLE. DAY.

Behind a huge glass window STUDENTS can be seen working in the ancient college library...

JUDE looks around the quadrangle...

From one of the archways a group of COLLEGE TUTORS appear...

JUDE watches them...

They disappear through another archway...

JUDE follows hesitantly...

63. INT. ARCHWAY/ BIBBLIOL COLLEGE. DAY.

JUDE hears footsteps echoing all around the dark stone corridor...

34

64. EXT. INNER QUADRANGLE/ BIBBLIOL COLLEGE. DAY.

JUDE walks into another open quadrangle...

The statue of an academic giant dominates the courtyard...

JUDE stares up at it reverently...

He doesn't hear the footsteps behind him. A pair of hands suddenly cover his eyes. JUDE knows who it is at once...

> JUDE
> Sue.

> SUE
> How do you know?

> JUDE
> You've got women's hands.

> SUE
> You'll have to do better than that.

JUDE wriggles out of her grasp...

> JUDE
> There you go.

> SUE
> Brute force doesn't count.

JUDE smiles happily...

> JUDE
> You've been following me.

> SUE
> I came to say goodbye.

JUDE is stunned by the news...

SUE looks nonchalant...

> SUE
> Aren't you going to introduce me to your friend?

JUDE's still in a daze. It takes him a moment to realise she means the statue...

> JUDE
> That's Ward.

> SUE
> How do you do Mr Ward?

She smiles at the statue primly...

35

JUDE and SUE walk down the busy street...

SUE admires the PASSERSBY in their colourful dresses...

JUDE looks troubled...

> JUDE
> Why are you leaving?

> SUE
> I haven't got anywhere to stay.

> JUDE
> What's wrong with where you are now?

> SUE
> I had a row with my landlady. She found one of my statues and threw it on the floor and stamped on it and ground the head to pieces with her heel. She made sure I lost my job as well.

> JUDE
> Where will you go?

> SUE
> I'm going to teach somewhere.

> JUDE
> You can teach here in Christminster.

> SUE
> There's no work. Everyone in this city's a teacher.

> JUDE
> I've got a friend who can help us. Mr Phillotson. I was his pupil in Marygreen.

> SUE
> Don't worry about me.

> JUDE
> I was going to look him up anyway. There's no harm in asking.

> SUE
> Why do you want me to stay?

> JUDE
> Because we've only just met.

Neither one speaks after that. They walk in reflective silence...

JUDE knocks and waits. He looks at SUE encouragingly...

A moment later the door opens. MR PHILLOTSON stands there with a candle in his hand...

It takes JUDE a moment to recognise him...

                    JUDE
          Mr Phillotson?

                    PHILLOTSON
          Yes.

                    JUDE
          My name is Jude Fawley.

                    PHILLOTSON
          How can I help you?

                    JUDE
          I was one of your pupils.

PHILLOTSON doesn't recognise him. The disappointment shows on JUDE's face. He feels even worse because SUE is there...

                    JUDE
          At Marygreen...

                    PHILLOTSON
          Yes. Of course you were. I thought your face looked familiar.

PHILLOTSON looks at SUE in the candlelight...

                    PHILLOTSON
          Are you an old pupil too?

                    JUDE
          No this is my Cousin Sue... Mr Phillotson you once showed me
          Christminster from the barn roof. The same day you left
          Marygreen. I came here because of you Sir. To become a
          University man.

PHILLOTSON seems to recollect something vague in his past. He looks at Jude more closely...

                    PHILLOTSON
          Well come in. Come in...

67. INT. MR PHILLOTSON'S HOUSE. NIGHT.

PHILLOTSON leads JUDE and SUE down a narrow corridor. They pass the schoolroom with desks and a blackboard...

68. INT. PARLOUR/ PHILLOTSON'S HOUSE. NIGHT.

JUDE, SUE and PHILLOTSON sit closely around the single lamp...

> PHILLOTSON
> ...I gave up the idea of University a long time ago. It took a
> while to forget the dream. But other dreams have replaced it.
> I'm very happy as a schoolmaster now.

> JUDE
> Sue's been looking for work as a teacher.

PHILLOTSON glances at SUE. She meets his gaze confidently...

> JUDE
> You've already had some experience haven't you Sue...

> SUE
> No Jude.

JUDE looks embarrassed...

> PHILLOTSON
> That makes it very hard to find work.

> SUE
> I was thinking of applying to a teacher's college.

> PHILLOTSON
> It's always a good idea. What I need for this school for example
> is a second year's transfer...

> JUDE
> What about an apprentice?

> SUE
> Jude.

She scolds him gently for pressing Mr Phillotson...

PHILLOTSON is gazing at SUE thoughtfully...

> PHILLOTSON
> Are you serious about being a teacher Sue?

> SUE
> Yes of course.

PHILLOTSON considers in silence...

> JUDE
> I'm sure it would be useful for both of you.

> PHILLOTSON
> I can't afford to pay you much...

                              SUE
          That doesn't matter.

SUE's eyes are full of excitement and enthusiasm.

PHILLOTSON smiles...

                          PHILLOTSON
          Alright then...

JUDE looks happiest of all...

69. INT. SCHOOL ROOM. DAY.

The SCHOOLCHILDREN sit around a gas stove to keep warm...

SUE is teaching them arithmetic on the blackboard...

70. INT. OUTSIDE THE SCHOOL ROOM. DAY.

JUDE and PHILLOTSON watch SUE teach. JUDE keeps looking at PHILLOTSON to see if he's
pleased with her...

PHILLOTSON watches SUE closely...

71. INT. JUDE'S LODGINGS. NIGHT.

JUDE strides around his small bare room, reciting his Greek Testament in a dramatic voice.
He's in a celebratory mood...

                              JUDE
          All hemin heis Theos ho pater, ex hou ta panta, kai hemeis eis
          auton, Kai heis Kurious Iesous Christos...

72. INT. EXHIBITION ROOM. DAY.

A view over the sunlit city of Jerusalem. It takes a moment to realise we're staring at a
backlit scale model in an exhibition room...

The CURATOR walks around the model city with a pointer in his hand, showing the
SCHOOLCHILDREN various places from the bible...

                          CURATOR
          Mount Moriah... The valley of Jehosophat... The City of Zion...
          Cavalry...

SUE and PHILLOTSON stand a little way back from the CROWD.

                              SUE
          How does anyone know what Jerusalem looked like at the time
          of Christ? I'm sure that man doesn't.

                          PHILLOTSON
          Of course he does. The model's copied from the best
          conjectural maps.

                              SUE
          Anyway why Jerusalem?   Why not Athens or Rome or
          Alexandria?

                              PHILLOTSON
          Because of what Jerusalem means to us. As Christians. Surely
          you must see that.

SUE doesn't respond. She looks annoyed.

                              PHILLOTSON
          Why are you so sceptical?

                              SUE
          I'm not. I was just pointing out... Jude!

SUE sees JUDE on the other side of the model city. He's crouching down, examining the
valley of Jehosophat. He looks up as she calls his name...

SUE leaves PHILLOTSON abruptly and joins her cousin by the Mount of Olives...

                              JUDE
          What a surprise...

                              SUE
          No it isn't. You knew I'd be here. You've been watching me all
          the time.

JUDE smiles happily...

                              SUE
          That's better. You looked so serious studying Jerusalem.

PHILLOTSON appears at SUE's shoulder again...

                              JUDE
          Mr Phillotson.

                              PHILLOTSON
          Jude. You cousin is such a clever girl she criticises all this
          unmercifully...

                              SUE
          Please don't call me a clever girl Mr Phillotson. There are too
          many of us about these days.

JUDE and PHILLOTSON are taken aback by her sharp sarcasm...

                              PHILLOTSON
          I didn't mean anything Sue...

                              SUE
          I know you didn't. Come on Jude, I think we've had enough of
          Jerusalem.

SUE takes JUDE by the hand and leads him out of the hall...

PHILLOTSON looks quietly crushed...

73. EXT. EXHIBITION HALL. DAY.

JUDE and SUE walk out of the exhibition building...

> SUE
> Why is it that men never let you finish a sentence. They interrupt at exactly the point when your argument is at its weakest...

> JUDE
> He didn't mean badly.

> SUE
> See you're doing it too.

JUDE grins...

> SUE
> What?

> JUDE
> You feel guilty.

> SUE
> No I don't. Why should I?

> JUDE
> You overreacted.

> SUE
> You didn't hear what he said.

> JUDE
> I know why he said it. He only wanted to impress you.

> SUE
> It's not a very clever way to go about it.

> JUDE
> He can't be clever. He's fond of you.

> SUE
> Well I'm fond of him too. It doesn't mean I go around patronising him. I don't feel at all guilty.

JUDE smiles softly...

> SUE
> Do you think I should apologise?

JUDE laughs at her and she laughs at herself...

41

74. EXT. CLOISTERS/ BIBBLIOL COLLEGE. DAY.

JUDE and SUE walk around the gloomy cloisters, past ghostly statues with their features eaten away by time...

JUDE holds a letter in his hand. He's concentrating as he walks...

SUE glances at him with a little smile...

> SUE
> How many more times do we have to walk round?

> JUDE
> Twice.

> SUE
> Is seven a magic number?

JUDE ignores her gently teasing...

> SUE
> I thought you weren't superstitious?

> JUDE
> Better to be safe.

They keep walking...

SUE mimics JUDE's earnest and serious expression...

She can't help teasing him...

She starts to recite in a low growl...

> SUE
> "All hemin heis Theos ho Pater, ex hou ta panta, kai hemeis eis auton..."

JUDE smiles slightly but keeps concentrating. He clutches his letter firmly in his hand...

75. INT. PORTER'S LODGE. DAY.

STUDENTS IN BLACK GOWNS crowd the porter's lodge...

JUDE is waiting for everyone to leave before he hands in his application...

The STUDENTS file out...

JUDE turns to SUE and holds up the letter...

> JUDE
> Will you kiss it for luck.

SUE looks at him with a warm affectionate smile...

SUE
No I'll kiss you for luck.

She pecks him gently on the cheek...

JUDE feels the moment strongly...

He looks into her eyes briefly and then turns and walks confidently towards the COLLEGE PORTER's cabin...

He hands in the letter...

JUDE
A letter for the Dean of Admissions...

76. EXT. STONEYARD. DAY.

The pouring rain has turned the stoneyard into a grey marshland. The MASONS work under leaking tarpaulins...

JUDE batters his block of granite harder and faster than anyone else...

77. EXT/INT. STAIRWAY/ JUDE'S LODGINGS. NIGHT.

JUDE skips down the rickety stairway. He's changed into his finest clothes...

78. EXT. SCHOOL HOUSE. NIGHT.

The rain veils the school house. The lights are on inside...

JUDE hurries towards the building through the downpour...

The lights go off. Two figures step out of the school house, sheltering under a single umbrella...

JUDE recognises them. He call out:

JUDE
Sue... Mr Phillotson...

His voice is drowned out by the rain. They don't hear him. They start to walk away in the opposite direction...

JUDE puts his hands to his mouth and is about to call out again when he sees something...

PHILLOTSON places his arm around SUE's waist to pull her closer under the umbrella. She gently removes his hand...

JUDE stares in curious silence...

PHILLOTSON says something to SUE. JUDE can't hear a word through the deafening rain. PHILLOTSON slips his arm around her shoulder more firmly and pulls her under the umbrella. This time SUE doesn't resist. She moves closer to him. PHILLOTSON's hand lingers on her back and then slips slowly around her waist...

SUE glances around briefly but doesn't see JUDE. The two of them walk on...

JUDE stares through the pouring rain, in crushed disbelief...

79. INT. JUDE'S ROOM. NIGHT.

The rain lashes against the window...

JUDE stares at the water patterns on the glass pane. He's still in a daze. He can't believe what he's just seen...

There's a knock on the door. JUDE doesn't answer...

> LANDLADY OFFSCREEN
> Mr Fawley?

JUDE still doesn't reply...

A letter is slipped under his door...

JUDE waits until the landlady's footsteps have disappeared. He walks over to the door and picks up the letter. The envelope has a College crest stamped on it...

> DEAN OF ADMISSIONS VOICEOVER
> Sir. I have read your letter with interest, and judging from your description of yourself as a working man, I think you will have a much better chance of success in life by remaining in your own sphere and sticking to your trade than by adopting any other course. That is what I advise you to do. Yours Faithfully, T Tetuphany, Dean of Admissions, Bibbliol College, Christminster...

JUDE tears the letter into pieces...

80. EXT. BIBBLIOL COLLEGE GATE. NIGHT.

Jude works by the light of the street lamps. With a piece of chalk he scrawls an inscription across the College entrance...

"I have understanding as well as you; I am not inferior to you; yea who knoweth not such things as these - Job xii. 3."

81. INT. PUBLIC HOUSE. NIGHT.

JUDE slouches over the beer wet table, noisy and drunk...

> JUDE
> ...I don't care a damn for any Provost, Warden, Principal, Fellow, or bloody Master of Arts. All I know is that I'd lick 'em on their own ground if they'd just give me the chance...

A small crowd of PUB REGULARS has gathered around to listen and laugh...

> TINKER TAYLOR
> I've always said there's more to be learnt outside a book than in.

                    UNCLE JOE
        Ay but can you say the creed in Latin man?

                       JUDE
              I can. I definitely can.

JUDE stands up unsteadily as if taking on a physical challenge...

A DRUNK UNDERGRADUATE stands up at a nearby table and hushes the whole pub...

                 DRUNK UNDERGRADUATE
        Excuse me! Quiet please! The gentleman in the corner is going
        to rehearse the Articles of his Belief, in the Latin tongue, for
        the edification of this company. Thank you.

There's mocking laughter all around...

                       JUDE
        Buy me a small Scotch cold and I'll do it straight off.

More laughter and incredulity. A glass of Scotch is passed from hand to hand until it
reaches JUDE. He downs it in one and scours his audience with wild drunken eyes, like a
mad prophet, waiting for silence...

When all is quiet JUDE begins in a slow resonant growl.

                       JUDE
        Credo in umum Deom, patrem omnipotentum Factorum coeli
        et terrae, visibilium omnium et invisibilium...

There's a surprised hush around the pub. Even though he's drunk there's a haunting
sonority and dignity in Jude's oration. His eyes blaze as he continues more intensely now:

                       JUDE
        Crucifixus etiam pro nobis: sub Pontio Pilato passus, et sepultus
        est. Et resurrexit tertia die, secundum scripturas...

Everyone is staring now. Even the mocking UNDERGRADUATES have shut up...

                       JUDE
        Et in spiritum sanctum, Dominum et vivificantem qui ex patre
        Filioque procedit...

JUDE stops. The CROWD looks at him in respectful silence. JUDE sneers at them haughtily...

                       JUDE
        You bloody fools! Which one of you knows if I said it right or
        not. It might have been the ratcatcher's daughter in double
        dutch for all you know...

JUDE turns away in disgust, at them, and at himself. He stumbles drunkenly out of the pub.
No-one speaks or moves. They just watch him in silence...

82. INT. SUE'S BEDROOM/ SCHOOL HOUSE. NIGHT.

SUE wakes up with a start. There's a knocking at her window. At first she thinks it's the rattle of the wind but then she hears Jude's voice calling out...

> JUDE OFFSCREEN
> Sue!... Sue!...

83. EXT. DOORWAY SCHOOL HOUSE. NIGHT.

JUDE stands outside, rainswept and bedraggled...

> SUE
> Jude... what's the matter?

The rain streams down his face...

> JUDE
> I've been drinking Sue... I can't help myself... I had to come...

84. INT. PARLOUR. NIGHT.

SUE helps JUDE lie down on an easy chair. He's shivering...

She takes off his filthy wet boots...

> JUDE
> I can do it...

She ignores him and rests his black and blistered feet on a cushion...

> SUE
> Are you hungry?

> JUDE
> No.

JUDE stares at her intensely...

> SUE
> You'll learn more than they can ever teach you. It may seem
> like empty words now but you don't need a double first from
> Christminster to do some good in the world...

> JUDE
> It isn't that...

SUE looks up curiously...

JUDE stares at her with wild eyes...

SUE feels uncomfortable in the silence...

> SUE
> You should try to eat something...

46

> JUDE
> He's too old for you.

SUE stares at him in silence...

It takes her a moment to realise what he means...

There's the briefest hint of emotion in her eyes....

She covers up quickly and resumes as if nothing has been said...

> SUE
> I'll bring your breakfast in the morning.

SUE slips away with an awkward smile...

JUDE is too ashamed to look at her...

85. INT. PARLOUR. DAY.

The rain starts up on the window...

JUDE wakes up with a headache. He looks around. At first he doesn't know where he is...

He sees his boots. They've been cleaned. He suddenly remembers...

JUDE stares at the door to SUE's bedroom. He knows he can't face her...

He picks up his boots and slips noiselessly out of the house...

86. EXT. ROAD OUT OF CHRISTMINSTER. DAY.

JUDE walks through the drizzle with his belongings in a sack. The view of Christminster fades behind him...

87. EXT. ROAD TO MARYGREEN. NIGHT.

The downpour is relentless. JUDE sleeps under the shelter of a rick...

88. EXT. MARYGREEN / INT AUNT DRUSILLA'S HOUSE. DAY.

JUDE walks through the village to AUNT DRUSILLA's house. He goes into the bakery.

JUDE stands before AUNT DRUSILLA. He looks tired and mud-spattered...

The old woman doesn't look at all surprised to see him. She snorts...

> AUNT DRUSILLA
> Out of work already?

89. INT. AUNT DRUSILLA'S HOUSE. DAY.

JUDE replaces the photograph of Sue on the mantlepiece...

> **AUNT DRUSILLA**
> Don't you be a fool about her Jude. Marrying that woman
> Arabella was about the worst thing you ever did. Until now...

> **JUDE**
> Don't say that Aunt...

> **AUNT DRUSILLA**
> I'll say it as much as it takes you to listen. Your parents couldn't
> live with each other. Nor could Sue's. They made each others'
> lives a living hell and left the two of you as good as orphans.

> **JUDE**
> We're a different generation.

> **AUNT DRUSILLA**
> With the same curse over your heads. The Fawley's are not
> made for marrying, and when they do nothing good comes of
> it.

> **JUDE**
> That's an old wives tale.

> **AUNT DRUSILLA**
> And since when have you stopped believing in them?

JUDE can't help smiling...

> **AUNT DRUSILLA**
> That's better. Now stop gawping at that picture.

90. INT. JUDE'S ROOM/ AUNT DRUSILLA'S HOUSE. DAY.

JUDE stares out of the window...

A mournful gale blows through the trees. The chimney and the eaves rattle. JUDE doesn't
hear a thing. He's in a world of his own...

90A. EXT. MARYGREEN. DAY.

JUDE walks through a grimy mud soaked street in Marygreen...

90B. EXT. COUNTRYSIDE/ MARYGREEN. DAY.

JUDE scurries up a hill, losing his footing several times. He shouts up at the top of the hill as
if it were an enemy he was hunting down...

90C. EXT. FIELD/ MARYGREEN. DAY.

The same field as in the opening scene. JUDE stands looking out over the valley...

90D. EXT. TRAIN. DAY.

The underside of the train whips past. Metal and smoke and speed...

SUE'S VOICEOVER FADES UP...

> SUE VOICEOVER
> Dearest Jude it was so good to hear from you at last and to see that you have put that silly town behind you. I'm writing to you from Melchester where Mr Phillotson and I have both moved.

90E. INT. TRAIN. DAY.

JUDE's face half disappears into the reflection of the speeding coutryside...

> SUE VOICEOVER (Cont)
> He is teaching at a new school and I am studying at a training college. The rules here are strict beyond belief and our visiting hours are limited, but I would do anything to see you again...

AT MELCHESTER

JUDE hurries down a gravel path towards the 15th Century mansion...

SUE waits for him in the courtyard. Her appearance has changed. She wears a gloomy uniform and her hair is tightly bunched up. Her eyes don't have their usual spark and joie de vivre...

JUDE clasps her hands affectionately and looks deeply into her eyes...

SUE is conscious that someone may be watching. She slips her fingers out of his grasp and holds his hands more discreetly, as if examining them...

                    SUE
          Your hands are rough Jude.

                    JUDE
          So would yours be if they held a mallet and chisel all day.

                    SUE
          I like them. They're noble hands.

She lets go of them gently...

                    JUDE
          What's wrong?

                    SUE
          It'll take me a while to get used to you again.

She smiles at him reassuringly...

92. INT. HOTHOUSE/ MELCHESTER. DAY.

JUDE and SUE walk through the hothouse...

Glorious coloured flowers and exotic plants make the glasshouse look almost primal...

[NB. DIALOGUE TO BE ADDED]

                    JUDE
          Is it that bad at the training school?

                    SUE
          I'm getting used to it. It's only another year. Mr Phillotson
          thinks he can get me a good job when I've finished.

                    JUDE
          How is he?

                    SUE
          He's been such a help.

                    JUDE
          I'm sure he has.

JUDE can't hide a trace of sarcasm in his voice...

SUE looks into his eyes curiously...

> SUE
> Are you being silly?

> JUDE
> No.

> SUE
> Jude?

> JUDE
> I didn't realise he took a long term interest in your future.

> SUE
> He's a friend.

> JUDE
> I'm sure he doesn't see it that way.

> SUE
> An old man like him?

> JUDE
> He isn't that old...

> SUE
> You said so yourself.

JUDE looks away...

SUE watches him closely...

> SUE
> What's the matter?

> JUDE
> I wish you'd be more open with me.

> SUE
> Alright he asked me to marry him.

> JUDE
> What did you say?

> SUE
> I said I'd think about it.

JUDE looks incredulous and irritated...

> SUE
> I'm sorry. Maybe I shouldn't have asked you to visit.

                            JUDE
          I'm not visiting. I've moved to Melchester.

There's a long silence...

Both are keenly aware of what's just been said...

Neither one speaks...

93. EXT. STONEWORKS/ MELCHESTER CATHEDRAL. DAY.

Monumental blocks of stone lie about the cathedral walls. The MASONS clamber over them
like worker ants. JUDE works at the highest point with an almost frightening intensity...

SUE watches him from down below...

94. EXT. MELCHESTER CATHEDRAL. DAY.

JUDE approaches like someone who's afraid of being stung...

SUE smiles cheerfully as if nothing's wrong...

                            SUE
          Tomorrow we have leave from three til nine.

It doesn't take long for JUDE's enthusiasm to return...

                            JUDE
          We can go to Wardour Castle.

                            SUE
          No ruins please Jude.

                            JUDE
          It's a classical building. Corinthian.

                            SUE
          I like the sound of Corinthian.

They're both smiling happily, reconciled again...

SCENES 95 & 96 CUT.

97. INT. WARDOUR CASTLE/ PICTURE GALLERY. DAY.

JUDE studies the devotional paintings up close. The other TOURISTS breeze past
disinterestedly...

SUE waits for JUDE to finish. Half of her is annoyed that he's taking so long, the other half
admires him for his willingness to learn. Finally she grabs him playfully under the arm and
pulls him away...

                            SUE
          That's enough showing off...

98. EXT. HILLS ABOVE WARDOUR CASTLE, DAY.

JUDE snaps off a long branch from a tree, and hands it to SUE as a walking stick...

> SUE
> It's going to be much harder to walk with this. It's all crooked.
> I'd have to be a hunchback.

> JUDE
> You're an urban miss through and through...

> SUE
> I grew up in the countryside same as you.

> JUDE
> Ah but you've lost your country ways.

SUE swipes him with the stick...

99. EXT. VIEW FROM THE HILLS, DAY.

A strong wind picks up scooped straws and hay stems in the fields below. It's as if a golden dust is passing through the valley...

JUDE glances at SUE...

SUE admires the open countryside. She enjoys the breeze on her face...

> SUE
> I'm never going to leave this spot. I'll stay here all my life.
> Nothing will ever change again.

> JUDE
> The Sun will go. And the wind.

> SUE
> I won't notice.

JUDE smiles as he watches her staring out blissfully...

> SUE
> It feels so good to be alone.

> JUDE
> What about me?

> SUE
> I don't count you Jude. You're part of my solitude. You can
> stand here beside me and we'll never speak a word.

SUE seems lost in the view...

> JUDE
> We should be getting home.

SUE ignores him...

                                    JUDE
                I think it's that way...

She holds his hand...

100. EXT. HILL DESCENT. DAY

SUE treads unsteadily down the hill. She can't stop her own momentum. She laughs
nervously. JUDE holds onto her so she doesn't slip...

                                    SUE
                I wish I hadn't thrown that stick away...

101. EXT. WOODLAND PATH. DAY.

SUE looks in pain. She stops. She can't go on...

                                    JUDE
                We'll miss the last train.

                                    SUE
                I can't Jude. I really can't...

                                    JUDE
                What about your school?

                                    SUE
                I need a rest, just ten minutes...

101A. EXT. WOODLAND CLEARING. DUSK.

SUE snores gently...

She's fast asleep under Jude's coat...

JUDE looks up through the trees...

The daylight is fading fast...

                                    JUDE
                Sue...

                                    SUE
                I'm awake...

                                    JUDE
                We have to go...

                                    SUE
                I'm awake...

She says it like she's sleepwalking...

She doesn't stir...

                                    JUDE
        Sue...

This time she doesn't answer...

JUDE looks around and throws a little stick at her...

She doesn't even stir...

JUDE gives up. He smiles to himself...

102. EXT. TRAIN TO MELCHESTER. DAY.

The train cuts across the Wessex downs. JUDE and SUE watch the countryside go by. A
horrible whistle shrieks through the glorious silence...

103. EXT. TRAINING COLLEGE BUILDING/ MELCHESTER. DAY.

JUDE watches SUE hurry down the gravel path...

The windows on each floor of the building are full of staring faces. The other GIRLS have all
gathered to see what happens to SUE for absconding.

A stern looking MATRON steps ominously out of the front door...

SUE leaves JUDE with a brave smile...

She strides towards the MATRON confidently as if she has nothing to be ashamed of...

103A. EXT. JUDE'S LODGINGS/ MELCHESTER. DAY.

JUDE steps his way past some LOAFERS into his boarding house...

104. INT. JUDE'S LODGINGS/ MELCHESTER. NIGHT.

An oil lamp burns dirty black spirals of smoke...

JUDE sits at his desk, reading...

A handful of pebbles rattles against his window...

JUDE gets up and pulls the curtains open...

In the dim streetlight he can just make out SUE's shivering form...

105. INT. STAIRWAY/ JUDE'S LODGINGS/ MELCHESTER. NIGHT.

SUE steps into the arc of JUDE's lamp. She is soaking wet from head to foot. Her clothes
are caked in thick mud. Her hair is wild and knotted...

                                    JUDE
        What have you done?

                                    SUE
        Walked across the deepest river in the land.

JUDE stares at her with concern and confusion...

                    SUE
          They locked me up for being out with you. I jumped out of a
          window and climbed a fence and crossed a stream...

She tries to smile but tears fill her eyes...

106. INT. JUDE'S LODGINGS. NIGHT.

SUE shivers by the fireside in her clinging dress...

                    SUE
          I can't get warm.

                    JUDE
          I'll borrow some clothes from the Landlady.

                    SUE
          No, don't let her know for God's sake!

                    JUDE
          Then you must wear some of mine...

JUDE opens a drawer and takes out a dark suit...

                    JUDE
          How about my Sunday suit?

He spreads it for her to see...

                    SUE
          It might be too small.

They both smile...

107. EXT. OUTSIDE JUDE'S LODGINGS. NIGHT.

SUE'S SILHOUETTE moves past the window...

JUDE forces himself to look away. He's shivering in the alleyway, waiting for her to finish
changing into his clothes...

108. INT. JUDE'S LODGINGS. NIGHT.

JUDE opens the door softly and walks into the room...

SUE sits in his arm chair, dressed in his suit, looking achingly small and fragile...

                    JUDE
          I brought you some brandy.

                    SUE
          No glass?

                    JUDE
        There's some in the cupboard. I'll have to clean them.

                    SUE
        Don't worry. I'll drink it like a man.

She takes a sip out of the bottle and coughs gently...

                    JUDE
        What will the school do?

                    SUE
        I don't care.

It's clear from her expression that she cares very much...

The fire crackles...

Her clothes dry by the fireside...

                    SUE
        I'll go back as soon as they're dry.

                    JUDE
        No it's late. Stay here tonight.

They look at each other...

A long silence...

                    SUE
        I wish I could get warm.

JUDE throws his winter coat over her tenderly...

He kneels down beside her...

                    SUE
        Thank you.

                    JUDE
        For what?

                    SUE
        For being here when I came.

She takes his hand gently...

Their fingers play...

Neither dares look into the others' eyes...

                    JUDE
        I'm glad you came to me...

                          SUE
              There's no-one else...

Both of them feel the moment keenly...

JUDE lets go of SUE's fingers...

                          JUDE
              I should let you sleep.

                          SUE
              Yes.

JUDE stands up...

SUE smiles goodnight and closes her eyes...

JUDE watches her...

SUE's eyes flutter open again. She catches him staring at her...

                          SUE
              I couldn't sleep.

JUDE smiles distractedly...

He keeps staring...

                          SUE
              Why are you looking at me like that?

                          JUDE
              Does it frighten you?

                          SUE
              No. I'm not afraid of any man.

                          JUDE
              Why not?

                          SUE
              Because no man will touch a woman unless she invites him to.
              Until she says by a look or a smile "come on", he's always afraid.
               If you never say it, or look it, he'll never come. You're the
              timid sex...

Another long silence...

They stare at each other...

JUDE can't speak of act...

                          SUE
              Shall I try again?

JUDE isn't sure what she means...

                           SUE
            Close my eyes and fall asleep...

JUDE can't tell if it's a request or a statement...

SUE smiles...

Her eyes flutter shut again...

JUDE stares at her for a moment...

Her eyes stay closed this time...

JUDE wants to fall at her feet and kiss her...

Instead he turns and walks away...

109. INT. FIREPLACE/ JUDE'S ROOM. NIGHT.

JUDE dries SUE's clothes over the fire. Steam from her still damp dress rises up the chimney...

JUDE looks irritated with himself...

SUE opens her eyes. JUDE has his back to her. He doesn't know that she's awake. She watches him with her eyes squinting half shut, in case he turns around...

110. EXT. MELCHESTER CATHEDRAL. DAY.

High up on the scaffolding JUDE is working on a gothic spire...

111. EXT. STONEWORKS/ MELCHESTER CATHEDRAL. DAY.

JUDE walks over to where PHILLOTSON is waiting for him.

                        PHILLOTSON
            Is she staying with you?

JUDE hesitates...

                           JUDE
            This is about her running away from the school?

                        PHILLOTSON
            And coming to you at night.

PHILLOTSON looks at him closely...

                        PHILLOTSON
            There have been rumours. She's been expelled from the
            school because of them.

                           JUDE
            That isn't fair.

                    PHILLOTSON
        Jude I want to be able to defend her against any scandal...

There's something almost pleading in his voice. It's as if he's asking for help...

JUDE stares back in silence...

                    PHILLOTSON
        I need to know what happened between you?

JUDE finally speaks...

                    JUDE
        Nothing happened.

                    PHILLOTSON
        Is that the truth?

                    JUDE
        So help me God...

The words don't come easily...

                    JUDE
        She stayed with me. But as a cousin. A sister.

PHILLOTSON looks at him gratefully...

                    PHILLOTSON
        We must both help her now.

JUDE nods gently and looks away...

112. INT. JUDE'S LODGINGS. DAY.

SUE looks up weakly as the door opens. Her eyes light up when she sees JUDE...

JUDE looks uncomfortable. SUE notices but says nothing...

                    JUDE
        Did you go to the school?

                    SUE
        Yes. They won't take me back. They think you and I had some
        kind of affair...

                    JUDE
        It'll blow over.

                    SUE
        They even suggested I marry you for the sake of my
        reputation.

She tries to say it lightly but doesn't pull it off...

There's an awkward silence...

                    JUDE
          I saw Mr Phillotson today. He said he would help you.

                    SUE
          I don't want Mr Phillotson's help.

She says it quietly, curiously, almost like a question...

                    JUDE
          He was anxious. He cares for you very much...

SUE doesn't understand this sudden change...

JUDE stares back in guilty silence...

                    SUE
          What is it?

                    JUDE
          I've never told you about my past.

                    SUE
          You've told me most of it.

                    JUDE
          But not all of it...

It takes JUDE a long time to continue...

                    JUDE
          I'm married Sue. I haven't seen her for years, but I am still
          married.

SUE looks stunned. She looks away. It takes her a long time to compose herself...

                    SUE
          Why are you telling me this?

                    JUDE
          Because it's the only obstacle.

                    SUE
          Obstacle to what? How self centred you are. I don't love you. I
          don't want to be your wife. I'm already engaged. What did
          you think I meant?

                    JUDE
          Sue don't...

                    SUE
          You misunderstood me Jude. You and I are cousins, friends.

A distant formal smile...

JUDE pleads with his eyes...

                            61

SUE

Don't look so serious. It's nothing. Just a misunderstanding.

JUDE keeps staring...

SCENE 113 CUT

114. INT. JUDE'S LODGINGS. DAY.

[NB DIALOGUE TO BE REVISED, LOCATION CATHEDRAL CLOISERS]

JUDE, SUE and PHILLOTSON together.

PHILLOTSON

You're our closest mutual friend Jude. We though you ought to be the first to know...

JUDE

Congratulations...

SUE's smiling cheerfully but she still won't look at JUDE...

JUDE

When did you decide?

PHILLOTSON

Well I'd been asking for months now but this time it was Sue's idea. I can give away your little secret can't I darling...

SUE smiles coyly...

JUDE

I know it's the right decision.

SUE

Jude helped me make up my mind.

PHILLOTSON

I know. And I'm eternally grateful.

JUDE

I hope my cousin will make you very happy Mr Phillotson.

JUDE says it with a charming smile...

PHILLOTSON smiles happily...

Only SUE feels Jude's stinging remark as it's intended...

SUE

Jude I have something to ask you...

She looks at him for the first time. There's a hint of anger in her eyes. She hides it with a sweet smile...

62

                                SUE
        Will you give me away? I have no other family here.

JUDE is struck...

He can't speak...

PHILLOTSON smiles gently, finding the whole scene touching, completely missing the undertone...

SUE stares at JUDE unflinchingly...

                                JUDE
        Of course I'll give you away. With all my heart.

He stares right back at her...

115. EXT. CHURCH OF ST THOMAS. DAY.

A bleak sky hangs over the drab looking church...

116. INT ANTECHAMBER/ CHURCH OF ST THOMAS. DAY.

SUE holds onto JUDE's arm as they wait for the Church doors to open...

She looks beautiful in her white wedding dress...

They can hear the murmuring of the congregation inside the main hall...

                                SUE
        You're "Father" you know, that's what they call the man who
        gives you away...

JUDE doesn't respond...

                                SUE
        Was it like this when you were married?

JUDE feels her sting deeply...

Behind the veil SUE's eyes fill with tears. Her quiet sarcasm hurts her as much as it hurts JUDE...

The organ sounds and the Church doors creak open...

JUDE and SUE walk through arm in arm...

117. INT. CHURCH HALL. DAY.

JUDE leads SUE down the nave towards the altar...

SUE keeps her hand firmly on his arm...

Smiling FACES stare at them from the aisles...

They walk in painful silence. Neither can bear to look at the other...

                                63

SUE's hand leaves JUDE's and takes PHILLOTSON's...

The voices of the choir and congregation pick up as SUE and PHILLOTSON kneel at the altar...

JUDE steps back...

118. INT. PUBLIC HOUSE. NIGHT.

JUDE drinks on his own in one of the closed compartments of the public house. He stares through the thick ground glass of the partition. Passing figures become shimmering patterns of colour, arms and limbs distorted and insubstantial as they drink and flirt and shout about the din...

JUDE downs his drink in one and gets up unsteadily to buy himself another...

Bevel edged mirrors line the bar. Bottles of drink, the colour of topaz, amethysts, and emeralds, sit on glass shelves. Lights glint and blind. Everything is reflected and refracted so that it's hard to know who's where or what's what...

JUDE's drunk too much. The pub is a dizzying blur of colour and noise. He pushes his way to the front of the bar...

The BARMAID walks off just as JUDE arrives to order his drink. She's off flirting with a PUNTER at the other end of the bar. JUDE is about to call her back angrily when he suddenly stops...

He catches a brief glimpse of her face, reflected in the mirrors, distorted by the lights...

JUDE thinks he recognises her. He walks closer, edging people out of the way, leaning on the bar for support...

The BARMAID lights the PUNTER's cigarette flirtatiously. She moves the match away from him to blow it out. Just then she sees JUDE. It's ARABELLA...

A huge smile lights up her face. She's genuinely, drunkenly pleased to see JUDE. She forgets all about the other PUNTER, and strides over to JUDE happily...

> ARABELLA
> What shall I get you Sir?

> JUDE
> Thanks Arabella, I've had enough.

> ARABELLA
> I'm free.

> JUDE
> You're supposed to be in Australia.

> ARABELLA
> You're supposed to be a Christminster Don.

The PUNTER Arabella was flirting with has pushed his way over jealously...

64

                              PUNTER
            Who's this then Bella?

                             ARABELLA
            My husband.

ARABELLA laughs loudly at the apologetic look on the PUNTER's face. JUDE laughs with her...

119. INT. BEDROOM/ INN. NIGHT.

JUDE finishes making love to ARABELLA with a drunken groan. He lies still in her arms.
ARABELLA holds his aching head and strokes his hair. She blows in his ear gently. She's
completely sober and in control...

                             ARABELLA
            Jude I have to tell you something...

JUDE groans incoherently and moves his face towards the comfort of her breasts...

                             ARABELLA
            Jude...?

He can't hear. She doesn't mind. It's easier to confess like this...

                             ARABELLA
            There's someone else. He's good to me. I'll leave in the
            morning before you get up. You won't mind will you?

ARABELLA keeps stroking her hair as if he were a sick child....

119A. EXT MARYGREEN. DAY

JUDE arrives in the village. AUNT DRUSILLA's bakery is closed down. A couple of the cottages
have become derelict.

120. INT. AUNT DRUSILLA'S BEDROOM/ MARYGREEN. DAY.

AUNT DRUSILLA lies in bed. She doesn't move. She looks pale as a corpse...

JUDE sits at her bedside...

                          AUNT DRUSILLA
            I'll lie here still as Lazarus and then I'll suddenly open my eyes...

Her voice is rasping but as always there's a sly tone to it...

                          AUNT DRUSILLA
            "Sue Bridehead you little fool"... I'll say it straight out... "You'll
            regret this marriage as much as that ox of a cousin of yours
            regretted his."

Her eyes roll mischievously towards JUDE...

JUDE stares at his dying Aunt. He fights the tears...

Are you crying for me or for your precious Sue you ninny?

JUDE can't help laughing...

121. EXT. GRAVEYARD/ CHURCH/ MARYGREEN. DAY.

There's a cawing of birds in the mist...

JUDE stands behind a group of OLD LADIES DRESSED IN BLACK. He stares morbidly into the grave as earth spatters over Aunt Drusilla's coffin. There are tears in his eyes...

JUDE looks away...

Through the mist he sees a carriage arriving outside the church yard. A WOMAN steps out and pays the DRIVER. She hurries over to join the congregation. It's SUE...

122. EXT. CHURCH LANE/ MARYGREEN. DAY.

JUDE and SUE walk deliberately slowly...

> JUDE
> Where are you staying tonight?

> SUE
> In Marygreen. I'm going back tomorrow.

The OLD WOMEN IN BLACK disappear up ahead...

> SUE
> I wish I'd seen her before she died.

> JUDE
> She was looking forward to seeing you too.

> SUE
> What did she say?

> JUDE
> That we both made bad husbands and wives...

SUE remains determinedly silent...

> JUDE
> Sue are you happy?

> SUE
> Of course I am. How can a woman be unhappy who's only
> been married eight weeks?

Her tone silences JUDE. They both walk faster now...

Up ahead the OLD LADIES IN BLACK reappear...

123. INT. JUDE'S BEDROOM/ MARYGREEN. NIGHT.

The pitiful cry of a wounded animal cuts through the silence...

JUDE walks over to the window with a lamp. All he can see is his own reflection in the glass. It's pitch black outside...

The piercing shriek shrills out again...

124. EXT. MARYGREEN. NIGHT.

JUDE walks through the forest with a lamp in his hand. It casts an eerie glow over the trees. The howling of the animal is getting closer...

125. EXT. RABBIT TRAP/ WOODLAND. NIGHT.

The tiny rabbit drags its trap behind it. The metal teeth have clamped shut over its hind leg and slowly stripped the leg bone off its flesh. The more the rabbit struggles, the more it rips its leg to pieces...

JUDE holds the squealing rabbit still, and smacks his fist across its nick, putting it out of its misery...

As the rabbit dies JUDE hears a faint gasp. He looks up. SUE stands by the trees, lit up by her lamp...

She stares at the dead animal sadly...

> SUE
> I'm glad you got here first... They shouldn't be allowed to set these steel traps...

> JUDE
> Did it keep you awake?

> SUE
> I was awake.

> JUDE
> Why?

> SUE
> I was thinking.

> JUDE
> Thinking about what?

> SUE
> Why do you ask me?

He walks closer. His face look determined in the lamp light...

> JUDE
> Because I want you to be happy.

                              SUE
          I am happy...

Her voice is weak. She moves the lamp away from her face so that he can't see her tears...

JUDE walks even closer until they're almost touching. He stares at the shadows hiding her eyes. He hears her start to sob gently...

                              SUE
          How can I be happy...

The tears wrack her body. JUDE takes her in his arms and holds her comfortingly. She buries her head in his neck and cries. JUDE hugs her closer. Involuntarily SUE starts to kiss his neck, weakly at first, but gradually more desperately, more passionately. JUDE tries to look into her eyes for confirmation but she won't let him. She finds his lips and kisses him deeply. JUDE reacts slowly he's so surprised. When he does she pulls away from him. JUDE tries to hold her but she slips away determinedly...

JUDE watches her lamp light disappear into the forest...

AT SHASTON

126. EXT. SHASTON HILL. DAY.

Painted Gypsy caravans line the ascent up to Shaston...

JUDE walks up the hill road...

> SUE VOICEOVER
> Dearest Jude I should never have written this letter and I beg
> you not to reply. Try to forget whatever happened at
> Marygreen. Even if it seemed right at the time it is wrong
> now...

GYPSY CHILDREN fight violently in the rubbish dumps...

127. EXT. SCHOOLYARD ROAD/ SHASTON. DAY.

The bell rings for the end of school...

> SUE VOICEOVER (Cont)
> Richard and I are husband and wife. Nothing can change that.
> Not your frustration nor my regret. Even if I made a mistake it
> is now irreversible...

A group of excited SCHOOLGIRLS in red pinafores charge down the street past JUDE...

128. INT. SCHOOL/ SHASTON. DAY.

JUDE waits in an empty school room...

The walls are lined with colourful childrens' drawings...

> SUE VOICEOVER (Cont)
> I've taken a decision and I have to stand by it. I will learn to
> love him. Help me Jude. Forget me Jude...

Outside in the corridor an OLD LADY finishes sweeping the floor...

JUDE listens to her footsteps disappear...

He looks around...

The childrens' pictures depict bright coloured suns; houses with crooked windows; stick
figure husbands and wives and babies...

JUDE sits at a piano...

He starts to tinkle loosely...

Slowly it turns into a tune...

He doesn't hear the quiet footsteps behind him...

A pair of hands covers his eyes...

> JUDE
> Sue.

                            SUE
          How did you know?

JUDE laughs cheerfully and keeps playing...

SUE sits next to him. She starts to play a different tune...

The tunes grow together in tempo...

It's part competition part improvisation...

They both play faster and faster...

SUE finally grabs JUDE's hand so he can't play anymore...

                            JUDE
          Cheat.

                            SUE
          Bad loser.

They look at each other...

Neither can speak for a moment...

                            SUE
          Did you get my letter?

                            JUDE
          Yes, but I never opened it.

SUE smiles gently. She seems pleased...

                            JUDE
          Don't worry. I haven't moved to Shaston this time...

                            SUE
          You say it like you've given up with me.

                            JUDE
          Do you blame me?

SUE looks hurt...

                            JUDE
          I'm here aren't I?

SUE takes his hands...

                            SUE
          Promise me you'll never stop trying Jude.

JUDE can't help smiling...

                    SUE
        That must sound terrible.

                    JUDE
        Yes it does.

                    SUE
        Will you promise? Even when I push you away?

                    JUDE
        I can't help myself.

She squeezes his hand gratefully...

There's a great sadness in her eyes...

                    SUE
        And I promise I'll hear you Jude. One day.

Suddenly there's a quiet knock on the door...

They both look around sharply...

PHILLOTSON stands by the door...

                    PHILLOTSON
        Jude...

JUDE stands up awkwardly...

                    PHILLOTSON
        Sue didn't tell me you were coming.

                    SUE
        I didn't know.

For a moment neither of them know how PHILLOTSON's going to react...

                    PHILLOTSON
        Well it's a wonderful surprise for both of us. How long are you
        staying?

                    JUDE
        My coach leaves in an hour.

                    PHILLOTSON
        But poor Sue has hardly had a chance to see you.

PHILLOTSON looks at SUE for the first time. She feels uncomfortable. She still doesn't know
what he's thinking...

                    PHILLOTSON
        Maybe you can persuade Jude to stay with us darling.

SUE turns to JUDE...

                    71

                                SUE
         Yes, you must...

JUDE forces a smile...

129. INT. DINING ROOM/ PHILLOTSON'S HOUSE. NIGHT.

JUDE and SUE and PHILLOTSON sit around a long table having supper...

PHILLOTSON reminisces as he eats...

                            PHILLOTSON
         ...And Jude was following me down the road, getting further
         and further away from Marygreen. I think he would have
         followed me all the way to Christminster if I hadn't seen him.
         Had we been to the Brown House Barn together before?

                                JUDE
         No.

                            PHILLOTSON
         I'm sure we had. On a class expedition?

                                JUDE
         I was never in your class.

                            PHILLOTSON
         Yes you were. I'm sure you were in my lower third. I
         remember distinctly...

                                SUE
         You didn't even remember who he was Richard when we came
         to you in Christminster.

She can't help the tone in her voice...

PHILLOTSON looks quietly crushed...

There's an embarrassing silence...

                                JUDE
         You recognised me very quickly though...

                            PHILLOTSON
         Yes I did...

PHILLOTSON smiles awkwardly. He can't continue. He looks deeply hurt...

JUDE feels sorry for him...

SUE's knife and fork scrapes loudly in the silence...

130. INT. GUEST ROOM/ PHILLOTSON'S HOUSE. NIGHT.

JUDE lies in bed, wide awake, listening in the dark...

From another part of the house he hears faint voices. They seem to be arguing...

JUDE climbs out of bed...

The voices are coming from downstairs...

JUDE opens the bedroom door so he can hear better...

The voices have stopped...

The corridor outside is pitch black...

Suddenly JUDE hears quiet footsteps climbing the stairs...

The arc of a gas lamp lights the corridor...

JUDE walks out to see who it is...

131. INT. CORRIDOR/ PHILLOTSON'S HOUSE. NIGHT.

PHILLOTSON hears JUDE and turns around...

They stare at each other across the corridor...

The gas lamp lights PHILLOTSON's face...

JUDE can just make out the tears in his eyes...

> PHILLOTSON
> Is everything alright?

His voice is steady and dignified but JUDE senses the effort...

> JUDE
> Yes.

PHILLOTSON forces a smile...

> PHILLOTSON
> Goodnight then.

> JUDE
> Goodnight.

PHILLOTSON disappears back into his room...

JUDE stays where he is...

He stares down the dark and silent stairway...

132. INT. STAIRWAY/ PHILLOTSON'S HOUSE. NIGHT.

JUDE edges his way down the stairs...

There's a flickering light coming from behind the kitchen door...

133. INT. KITCHEN/ PHILLOTSON'S HOUSE. NIGHT.

JUDE pushes open the kitchen door...

There's no-one there...

A lamp burns on the table...

> JUDE
> Sue?

JUDE suddenly hears a rustling noise...

It seems to be coming from the kitchen closet...

He walks over slowly...

> JUDE
> Sue?

There's still no reply...

JUDE slowly open the closet door...

134. INT. CLOSET/ KITCHEN. NIGHT.

SUE is hunched in the cramped closet like a frightened animal. She's laid out a blanket and a pillow on the dusty floor. A single candle lights up the cobwebs and dirt. SUE has made herself a nest. She stares up at JUDE with haunted eyes...

> SUE
> Please go away...

JUDE stares at her in stunned silence...

> JUDE
> What are you doing?

SUE doesn't reply...

She looks as if she's about to cry...

JUDE crouches down and crawls into the cupboard beside her...

She draws up her legs to make room...

JUDE sits beside her in silence...

In the candlelight a beautiful brown spider crawls up its web...

SUE stares at it...

The tears finally come...

Her voice shakes...

> SUE
> I wish he would beat me or be faithless or do something to justify my feeling like this... What's wrong with me Jude?

> JUDE
> Nothing.

> SUE
> He's the kindest gentlest man...

She can't continue...

JUDE waits..:

> SUE
> It's torture for me to be with him...

JUDE takes her in his arms...

He holds her tightly as she sobs...

He kisses her hair tenderly...

135. EXT. SCHOOL/ SHASTON. DAY.

The trees shake in the wind...

We hear Girls' voices repeating their Latin conjugations...

JUDE watches PHILLOTSON through the classroom window...

He's teaching a class of eight year old girls...

He taps the blackboard with a stick...

136. INT. CLASSROOM/ SHASTON. DAY.

PHILLOTSON sits behind his desk...

He struggles to control his emotions...

There's a tragic dignity about him...

> PHILLOTSON
> I have a wife I love, who not only doesn't love me, but... I disgust her... Every time I try to touch her...

PHILLOTSON can't look at JUDE...

                    PHILLOTSON
You heard us last night?

                    JUDE
Yes.

                    PHILLOTSON
I found her sleeping in the kitchen closet. She felt more
comfortable with the spiders and cobwebs...

PHILLOTSON tries to laugh ironically but he's closer to tears...

                    PHILLOTSON
And then this morning she asked if she could leave me... to live
with you...

PHILLOTSON looks at JUDE for the first time...

JUDE doesn't know what to say. His elation is mixed with pity for his rival...

                    PHILLOTSON
I won't oppose it... if that's what you want.

                    JUDE
Yes it is.

PHILLOTSON takes a moment to gather himself. His voice is cracked...

                    PHILLOTSON
I've always noticed something extraordinary between the two
of you. I tried to tell myself it was because you were cousins...
but it's more than that... Sometimes I think you're one person
split in two...

JUDE says nothing...

                    PHILLOTSON
You knew all along she'd made a mistake marrying me?

                    JUDE
Yes.

                    PHILLOTSON
But you did nothing to stop us?

                    JUDE
No.

                    PHILLOTSON
No. Nor did I.

PHILLOTSON looks away as the tears come...

PHILLOTSON lifts SUE's suitcases off the carriage and hands them to JUDE...

The two men stare at each other briefly...

PHILLOTSON turns to SUE...

> PHILLOTSON
> I'll check when I get back home to see if you've forgotten anything.

> SUE
> I don't think I have. Thank you Richard.

She can't help looking and sounding apologetic...

> PHILLOTSON
> What time is your train Jude?

> JUDE
> It leaves in five minutes.

SUE keeps looking at PHILLOTSON, hoping that somehow he can forgive her...

> PHILLOTSON
> Do you need a hand with the luggage?

> JUDE
> We'll be fine. Thank you.

PHILLOTSON's face is taut with effort...

The pain isn't very far away...

He turns to SUE...

> PHILLOTSON
> Goodbye Dear.

SUE puts her arms around him and kisses him gratefully on the cheek...

She holds onto him for a moment...

PHILLOTSON pushes her away gently...

> PHILLOTSON
> I think I can hear your train.

137 EXT. TRAIN WHEELS. DAY.

JUDE and SUE are together in the train...

The wheels spin faster and faster until they're almost invisible...

AT ALDBRICKHAM AND ELSEWHERE

<u>137A. EXT. SEA/ SANDBOURNE. DAY.</u>

Bare feet running through the waves and foam...

We hear JUDE and SUE's laughter...

<u>137B. EXT. BEACH/ SANDBOURNE. DAY.</u>

JUDE and SUE walk away from the sea. They carry their shoes in their hands...

<u>137C. EXT. POV SANDBOURNE. DAY.</u>

The heavy rain pelts down...

JUDE is repairing the slate roof of a seaside house...

He's drenched. It's almost impossible to work in the downpour...

The wind blows the drizzle in his eyes...

In the distance the sea is grey and rainswept. The sky is almost black...

JUDE suddenly notices someone watching him down below...

It's SUE...

She stands by the date, under an umbrella, veiled by the rainfall...

She looks still and ghostly...

JUDE stop working and stares at her...

She smiles at him adoringly, oblivious to the downpour...

JUDE's face lights up...

They stare at each other through the falling rain, in silent communication...

<u>137Ci. EXT. BLIZZARD. DAY.</u>

The snow blows at us like thick clouds of smoke...

<u>137D. INT. TRAIN TO ALDBRICKHAM. DAY.</u>

JUDE and SUE together...

JUDE rests his head against the window, trying to get some sleep...

His eyes crack open every time the coach hits a bump...

The carriage is crammed full of PEOPLE...

<u>137Di. EXT. ALDBRICKHAM. DAY.</u>

A slower movement now across rows of drab back to back houses...

The room is bare and empty...

JUDE and SUE have just moved in...

They lean against the window looking down at the street below...

Some tattered pieces of furniture are being carried into the house by WORKMEN...

> JUDE
> This time we'll stay. I promise.

SUE runs her finger across the dust on the window ledge...

> SUE
> I used to look out of the window at Shaston and cry so hard
> the teardrops would fall on the window sill. I drew circles in
> ink around each one to remind myself how unhappy I was.

SUE smiles gently...

> SUE
> It doesn't matter where we are or where we go. I'm happy
> Jude.

SUE breathes on the window pane until it mists up. She starts to draw a picture with her finger...

138. INT. PUBLIC HALL/ ALDBRICKHAM. DAY.

A CROWD are packed into the small sweltering hall. JUDE and SUE are squeezed near the back. They don't mind the crush and the heat. They're too involved in the debate. SUE's face is damp with sweat. Her eyes shine brightly as she listens...

> LECTURER
> ...The ideals of religion are negative: "Thou shalt not"
> predominates over "Thou Shalt". The threat of hell
> predominates over the promise of heaven...

The LECTURER is interrupted by cries of "Shame, shame"...

> HECKLER
> Get to the point!!

> LECTURER
> The point is that the negative has become a law written in
> stone, and we are too scared to live...

There are more cries of "Shame"...

SUE joins in vigorously with those who cry "Let him speak"...

> LECTURER
> Morality has to include the human as well as the religious part
> of our education.

79

                    HECKLER
          There's no difference!

                    SUE
          Of course there is...

SUE's voice is drowned in the general commotion...

                    HECKLER
          There has to be common public morality...

                    SUE
          Who decides what it is!?

                    HECKLER
          We have Church laws...

                    SUE
          Written centuries ago...

The LECTURER joins in too...

                    LECTURER
          The common public morality has to be qualified by people's
          right to choose for themselves...

More shouting...

JUDE watches SUE. She's completely absorbed in the debate...

139. EXT. PETTICOAT LANE/ ALDBRICKHAM MARKET. DAY.

The street is lined with second hand clothes. Suits and coats dangle from washing lines.
They tremble in the wind like hung men...

JUDE and SUE continue the debate as they walk through the market...

                    SUE
          ...Domestic laws should take into account different
          temperaments.

                    JUDE
          For example?

                    SUE
          I may want to live with a man but only as a friend.

                    JUDE
          That may not be fair on the man.

                    SUE
          Because there are no precedents. His pride is hurt.

                    JUDE
          But you'd want to marry someone you love?
                         80

                    SUE
Why do people have to be told to love each other by someone
else. That's all marriage is. It's a Government Stamp; a license
to love.

                    JUDE
But if we could wouldn't you want to get married?

                    SUE
I'd run a mile if you had a piece of paper that forced me to
love you.

JUDE has no answer...

They walk in silence...

The suits and coats on the hanging lines swing with the wind...

140. INT. LIVING ROOM/ JUDE & SUE'S HOUSE. NIGHT.

SUE leans over the table. She holds a coin in her hand...

                    SUE
          A little closer.

                    JUDE
          No.

                    SUE
          Please...

SUE pleads pretty and helpless...

JUDE grumbles and pushes the glass of beer nearer her...

SUE concentrates...

She bounces the coin off the table and tries to get it in the glass...

She misses completely...

JUDE laughs triumphantly...

                    JUDE
          Drink up...

                    SUE
          I get a second chance...

                    JUDE
Stop arguing for once and drink...

SUE sips the beer reluctantly...

81

JUDE
You love it you liar...

SUE pulls one of her faces and makes him laugh...

141. INT. BEDROOM/ JUDE AND SUE'S HOUSE. NIGHT.

JUDE follows SUE into the bedroom cheerfully...

He throws his arms around her and hugs her from behind...

SUE struggles gently and slips out of his grasp...

JUDE looks hurt...

                    SUE
What?

                    JUDE
All you have to do is say no. You don't have to slip away like
that.

                    SUE
Then don't touch me like that.

                    JUDE
It's just affection Sue.

                    SUE
As a prelude to something else.

                    JUDE
"Something else". What "something else"? I don't think either
of us knows the meaning of the word...

SUE looks deeply hurt...

JUDE regrets it at once...

                    JUDE
I'm sorry...

SUE nods as if to say she accepts his apology. She's too upset to speak...

                    JUDE
I'm sorry Sue... It's just that I want everything to be perfect
between us...

                    SUE
And isn't everything perfect?!

Her eyes blaze...

                    JUDE
Of course it is...

                                SUE
          Didn't we laugh today? Didn't we drink? Didn't we talk?

                                JUDE
               Sue...

                                SUE
          I'm not ready Jude. Do you understand?

There are tears in her eyes...

                                JUDE
               I'll try...

142. EXT. BACK YARD/ JUDE AND SUE'S HOUSE. DAY.

The back yard has been turned into a work area...

JUDE is bent over a headstone, chiseling an inscription...

SUE appears behind him with a mischievous smile...

JUDE concentrates on his work...

                                SUE
               What are you writing?

                                JUDE
               Whatever his wife wants.

                                SUE
               Here lies my husband Peter Porter aged 51. He tormented me,
               he cheated on me, and he never gave me enough money to
               buy clothes...

                                JUDE
               Sue he's dead.

                                SUE
               He can't hear me.

There's a knock on the door, inside the house...

They both laugh as if it's a ghostly apparition...

                                JUDE
               Tell him I'll have his headstone ready in an hour.

143. EXT. JUDE AND SUE'S HOUSE. DAY.

SUE opens the front door. There's no sign of anyone. SUE looks around the street...

JUDE arrives, rubbing his hands on his overalls...

                                JUDE
               Who was it?

83

SUE keeps staring out at the street. JUDE has a look. There's no-one there...

> JUDE
> It was a ghost.

He smiles cheerfully...

144. INT. JUDE AND SUE'S BEDROOM. NIGHT.

SUE sleeps in the bed. JUDE sleeps on the floor.

A knock on the door downstairs wakes them both up.

JUDE goes downstairs to see who it is...

145. EXT. OUTSIDE JUDE AND SUE'S HOUSE. NIGHT.

ARABELLA stands there, shivering in the cold...

JUDE looks stunned...

> JUDE
> Arabella...

> ARABELLA
> I didn't want to come...

Her voice is choked...

> ARABELLA
> I'm in terrible trouble Jude... I have to talk to you...

JUDE looks up...

SUE is watching him from the window...

ARABELLA sees her too...

> ARABELLA
> Maybe it would be easier if we met somewhere else. I don't
> want to cause any trouble...

JUDE is too dazed to think straight...

> JUDE
> Yes...

He looks up again...

SUE is still staring out of the window...

> ARABELLA
> I'm staying at the Temperance Hotel...

146. INT. JUDE AND SUE'S BEDROOM. NIGHT.

JUDE opens the door. SUE is in bed. She won't look at him...

> JUDE
> It was Arabella. She's in trouble.

> SUE
> What kind of trouble?

> JUDE
> I don't know. She wants to talk to me.

> SUE
> Can't she talk outside.

> JUDE
> She wants me to go to her hotel.

> SUE
> That's convenient.

> JUDE
> I have to help her Sue.

> SUE
> Why? She's not your wife.

> JUDE
> Nor are you.

A beat.

> SUE
> But she's going to give you what you want.

JUDE turns to leave...

> SUE
> Jude?!

JUDE hesitates. He hears her slipping out of the sheets. He hears her bare feet on the creaking wood...

> SUE
> If you go don't ever come back...

JUDE turns and faces her...

She stares at him in the darkness...

> SUE
> Can't you see what she's doing?... There is no trouble. She
> wants you back...

85

                        JUDE
         But do you want me?

SUE stares at him in silence...

                        JUDE
         Do you want me Sue?

SUE finally nods. That's all she can do...

JUDE takes her hesitantly in his arms. She doesn't resist. He kisses her gently on the neck, and on the cheeks...

Slowly the smell of her consumes him. The kisses become more passionate...

                        JUDE
         I'm sorry Sue... I'm sorry...

He keeps apologising as he feels himself losing control...

He breathes in her scent...

His heavy hands run up and down her back...

He falls to his knees and kisses her thighs passionately...

                        SUE
         No Jude...

                        JUDE
         What?!

                        SUE
         Slow down... please...

Her eyes implore...

She kneels down beside him and holds his face gently...

Her fingers move like butterflies across his cheeks...

Her touch calms him down...

JUDE is still now...

SUE kisses him on each eyelid and then softly on the lips...

JUDE closes his eyes...

                        JUDE
         You don't have to do this.

                        SUE
         I want to. But you have to help me. I don't know what I'm
         doing. I only pretend...

She laughs shyly and starts undoing her nightgown...

JUDE opens his eyes and looks at her...

>   SUE
> Close your eyes. There isn't much of me to look at...

JUDE keeps staring...

>   SUE
> Do I talk too much?

>   JUDE
> No.

SUE hesitates as she's about to slip the nightgown off her shoulders...

JUDE does it for her, gently...

He stares at her beautiful white body...

>   SUE
> You too, otherwise it's not fair...

There's an eagerness and playfulness about her. Her innocence is still there but the fear has gone...

JUDE takes his shirt off. His skin in shiny with sweat...

SUE lies down on her back slowly.   She looks up at JUDE for confirmation...

JUDE can't help smiling...

>   SUE
> I'm doing it all wrong aren't I?

>   JUDE
> No.

He looks at her lovingly as she lies on her back and waits for him...

>   SUE
> I'm intellectualising...

SUE closes her eyes...

JUDE hesitates...

>   SUE
> Kiss me before I start talking again...

JUDE lies on top of her...

She arches up and responds...

147. INT. KITCHEN/ JUDE AND SUES' HOUSE. DAY.

SUE is cooking breakfast...

JUDE walks down the stairs with a big grin on his face...

> SUE
> Don't look so pleased with yourself...

SUE pulls one of her prim faces...

> SUE
> I'm making you bacon and sausage and eggs.

> JUDE
> Why?

> SUE
> Because you think you deserve it.

JUDE laughs at her playful sarcasm...

> SUE
> There's a letter for you, on the table...

JUDE picks it up. As soon as he sees the writing on the envelope his expression changes. He puts the letter in his pocket...

> SUE
> Aren't you going to open it?

> JUDE
> I'll read it later...

> SUE
> Jude I know who it's from...

JUDE opens the letter...

ARABELLA'S VOICEOVER FADES UP...

> ARABELLA VOICEOVER
> Dear Jude. I'm writing with this news because I never got the chance to talk to you...

147A. EXT. VIEW FROM THE TRAIN. DAY.

An ugly urban landscape is reflected in the window...

As the train moves faster and faster the reflections fade and we see the face of a LITTLE BOY staring out...

148. INT. TRAIN CARRIAGE. DAY.

A small pale BOY sits in the gloom of the third class carriage. He has large frightened eyes and wears a white woolen cravat. A key is suspended from his neck. His ticket is stuck in his hat...

> ARABELLA VOICEOVER (Cont)
> The fact is that though I never informed you before, there was a boy born of our marriage, eight months after I left you...

149. EXT. TRAIN. DUSK.

The train hurtles through the bleak countryside...

> ARABELLA VOICEOVER (Cont)
> So far he has been with my parents in Sydney, but their situation has changed. They can no longer afford him, and nor can I...

150. INT. TRAIN CARRIAGE. NIGHT.

The other PASSENGERS stare at the boy...

He doesn't dare look back. His eyes are fixed on his reflection in the train window...

> ARABELLA VOICEOVER (Cont)
> I thought that with your situation more settled now, you might keep him. He is lawfully yours, I swear...

151. EXT. ALDBRICKHAM TRAIN STATION. NIGHT.

In the distance the lights of the train appear...

JUDE and SUE wait on the platform.

> JUDE
> I don't even know if he's mine.

> SUE
> Don't day that.

> JUDE
> If we were better off it wouldn't make any difference...

> SUE
> It shouldn't make any difference anyway.

The train lights get closer...

JUDE puts his arm around SUE...

> JUDE
> We'll do our best for him won't we?

> SUE
> Of course we will.

The noise is deafening. White steam fills the platform as the train comes to a slow stop...

JUDE and SUE watch nervously...

The LITTLE BOY emerges from the carriage. He walks towards them, head down, carrying his suitcase in his hand...

He looks up at JUDE timidly...

                              JUDE
          Are you Jude Fawley?

                              BOY
          Yes sir.

JUDE looks frozen...

SUE is the first to respond to the BOY...

                              SUE
          This is your father, and my name's Sue...

She bends down and hugs him and fusses over him as if she's known him all her life...

                              SUE
          We're so glad you came. How was your journey?

                              BOY
          Fine thank you.

                              SUE
          You must be starving. I don't know what you like but I guessed
          chicken...

The smile comes back to JUDE's face...

152. INT. BEDROOM/ JUDE AND SUE'S HOUSE. NIGHT.

The BOY lies asleep, pale and sickly, wrapped in blankets...

JUDE and SUE stand over him...

                              SUE
          What Arabella says is true... He's yours... I can see you in him...

SUE looks at the boy sadly...

                              SUE
          But the other half is her...

JUDE puts his arm around SUE comfortingly...

                              SUE
          Jude I wish he was ours... just ours...

JUDE pulls her closer to him...

                              SUE
                  We'll bring him up as if he were...

153. EXT. HAUNTED HOUSE/ FAIR. DAY.

The QUEUE pushes its way through he turnstiles...

JUDE lifts the BOY up so he can see the colourful facade of the haunted house...

Black castles and mists and ghostly apparitions are painted in chocolate box colours...

SUE pays for their tickets. Her stomach is bulging. She's pregnant...

154. INT. HAUNTED HOUSE. DAY.

JUDE and SUE and the BOY walk along a narrow ramp with rope on both sides...

It's dark inside the haunted house but daylight shows through cracks in the cardboard
walls. It's a cheap building and a cheap show...

                              JUDE
                  Does anything happen?

                              SUE
                  Shhh...

Up ahead a light comes on and fluorescent paper ghosts on sticks start to spin round and
round...

JUDE laughs at the tacky effect...

                              SUE
                  It's not funny Jude. It's frightening.

She gestures towards the BOY. He's staring intensely...

                              SUE
                       (Whispering to JUDE)
                  Some of us have got imaginations.

The light goes off and the ghosts disappear...

Eerie piano music tinkles out of the darkness...

                              SUE
                  Are you scared Juey?...

                           LITTLE JUDE
                  No.

                              SUE
                  Shall we carry on.

She takes LITTLE JUDE's hand...

                              91

                    SUE
          You'll protect me won't you?

                         LITTLE JUDE
          If I can.

Fake embers start to glow at their feet. Skeletal hands stick out of iron grills...

                    JUDE
          Look we're in hell...

SUE scowls at JUDE...

He holds up his hands in surrender...

                         LITTLE JUDE
          Mother look...

Up ahead three murderous faces appear out of the dark as if by magic...

                    JUDE
          How do they do that?

                    SUE
          They seem almost alive...

More faces appear all around them, mouths open in silent screams, glowing red and gold and orange...

                    SUE
          I wonder what would happen if I touched them.

                    JUDE
          Why don't you?

                    SUE
          Because it says not to.

                    JUDE
          You baby.

JUDE pushes her closer to the faces...

SUE squeals and wriggles out of his grasp...

LITTLE JUDE smiles appreciatively at his father's joke...

                    SUE
          You two are as bad as each other...

SUE pulls a face and walks off...

LITTLE JUDE looks at his father conspiratorially...

SUE suddenly screams as she walks into a giant cobweb...

JUDE is in hysterics...

A dozen papier mache spiders suddenly fall from the ceiling and dangle all around them...

155. INT. JUDE AND SUE'S HOUSE. NIGHT.

The sound of Sue's screaming fills the house...

JUDE stands by the bedroom door...

LITTLE JUDE appears at the top of the stairs...

> JUDE
> There's nothing to be frightened of... Come here...

JUDE takes the boy in his arms...

> JUDE
> It's a present from God...

Through the crack in the door they watch SUE lying on a bloodstained bed. She screams in agony as the DOCTOR and the MIDWIFE help her give birth...

LITTLE JUDE stares in silence...

> LITTLE JUDE
> How can it be from God if there's so much blood?

> JUDE
> It's special blood.

> LITTLE JUDE
> Why is Mother in pain?

> JUDE
> Don't worry. It's good pain. You'll see...

SUE starts screaming again...

155A. EXT. YARD/ JUDE'S HOUSE. DAY.

The NEWBORN BABY lies on its back twitching its arms and legs...

JUDE, SUE and LITTLE JUDE watch it in silence...

The baby starts to cry...

SUE looks at LITTLE JUDE tenderly...

> SUE
> Go on...

LITTLE JUDE hesitantly picks the BABY up and puts her over his shoulder...

The BABY stops crying at once...

93

LITTLE JUDE walks around with her. He looks pleased...

156. INT. CHURCH/ VILLAGE OUTSIDE ALDBRICKHAM. DAY.

The Ten Commandments dominate the chancel end of the Church. The stones are crumbling from damp...

JUDE has erected a platform on some scaffolding. He is restoring the lettering on the second tablet. SUE works next to him. She paints the letters...

LITTLE JUDE sits on one of the pews. He's looking after his BABY SISTER...

Suddenly the Church doors open loudly...

JUDE and SUE turn around...

A group of OLD LADIES DRESSED IN BLACK hover at the entrance...

JUDE and SUE carry on working. They hear the OLD LADIES whispering...

> SUE
> They don't approve...

The OLD LADIES disappear just as suddenly as they arrived...

> JUDE
> They're making sure we don't rub the "Not"s from the Ten Commandments.

> SUE
> I don't blame them. You're a famous reprobate after all.

They both try to smile...

157. INT. CHURCH. EVENING.

The whole family sits on a canvas sheet at the foot of the scaffolding. SUE breastfeeds her child. JUDE cuts some bread for his son...

The big church door open loudly once again...

SUE and JUDE look at each other anxiously...

TWO MEN IN SUITS hover at the entrance...

JUDE gives LITTLE JUDE his bread and gets up to see what his employers want...

SUE carries on breastfeeding. There's a calm and resigned look in her eye...

JUDE looks at the TWO MEN with a curious smile...

> JUDE
> The work's going fine Mr Willis. As you can see.

> MR WILLIS
> Jude I'm sorry... I'm going to have to get someone else to finish it for you...

> JUDE
> Why?

> MR BILES
> Some of the parishoners have complained...

> JUDE
> About what?

> MR BILES
> You never told us you weren't married.

> JUDE
> I never realised it was a necessary qualification for a stonemason.

JUDE stares at the man coldly...

> MR WILLIS
> I'll pay you for the week's work of course...

JUDE looks away in disgust...

At the other end of the Church SUE smiles at LITTLE JUDE reassuringly...

158. EXT. BACK YARD/ JUDE AND SUE'S HOUSE. DAY.

The AUCTIONEER stands on a chest of drawers. Beneath him every item of Jude and Sue's furniture is on sale. The BIDDERS are crowded in the courtyard...

> AUCTIONEER
> Now the next lot: two pairs of pigeons all alive and plump - a nice pie for someone's Sunday Dinner...

There's laughter as the AUCTIONEER holds up the bird cage...

159. INT. JUDE AND SUE'S BEDROOM. DAY.

The laughter downstairs can be heard faintly in the bedroom...

The room is completely bare now. JUDE and SUE sit on their one suitcase of belongings. SUE tries to hush the crying BABY...

LITTLE JUDE stares out of the window at the yard below.

> SUE
> It's going to be like this everywhere we go. As soon as people find out we're not married...

                                JUDE
            We'll move on. We'll move somewhere where nobody knows
            us and if they find out we'll move on again. And again. And
            again. As long as it takes the world to change.

He's determined to keep her spirits up...

                                JUDE
            We've done nothing wrong Sue. You're the one who taught
            me that.

There's the sound of more laughter down below...

160. EXT. COUNTRY ROAD. DAY.

It's pouring with rain. JUDE walks with a hood over his head. He's soaking wet. He coughs
unhealthily...

SUE sits in the cart with her children. She holds a piece of canvas over herself and LITTLE
JUDE and the BABY GIRL...

JUDE steadies the horse through the thick mud...

161. EXT. ROADWORKS. DAY.

An endless row of WORKERS line the roadside, evenly spaced, hammering away at rocks. It's
a relief work scheme. We see JUDE amongst them. He work like an automaton. The master
mason breaks stones for roadbuilding...

162. EXT. KENNETBRIDGE FAIR. DAY.

The spires of Christminster look as if they've crumbled and melted...

A huge knife cuts a tower and dome off the view...

We realise the cityscape is made of dough. These are Christminster Cakes.

JUDE wraps up a slice of cake...

SUE collects the money off the CUSTOMER with a grateful smile. She's pregnant again...

JUDE and SUE watch the CUSTOMER walking away. They seem to be doing less well than the
neighbouring snack barrows. They watch the other queues enviously...

                                SUE
            Maybe our Christminster cakes have an archaic taste to them.

JUDE smiles weakly. He looks dejected...

                                SUE
            Juey!

SUE looks around for LITTLE JUDE and her BABY...

They're nowhere to be seen...

                            SUE
          Juey!

SUE begins to look worried...

                            JUDE
          Juey!

LITTLE JUDE appears from under one of the tables, carrying his two year old SISTER on his back...

                            JUDE
          Don't just disappear like that. Tell us where you're going.

LITTLE JUDE looks apologetic...

                            JUDE
          Take care of your sister.

                            SUE
          Jude there's a customer coming...

Across the muddy field a LADY dressed in black approaches...

It's only as she gets closer that JUDE realises who it is...

SUE also recognises her at once...

ARABELLA smiles as she flounces towards their stall...

                            ARABELLA
          How do you do Mrs Fawley. We haven't met properly. Arabella
          Don.

SUE nods coolly...

ARABELLA looks JUDE up and down...

                            ARABELLA
          You look sick.

                            JUDE
          Thank you.

ARABELLA examines the cakes next...

                            ARABELLA
          There's even gables and little windows. How very sweet. Still
          harping on about Christminster Jude?

SUE looks more offended than JUDE...

                            ARABELLA
          If Christminster was a woman neither of us would have had
          him...

                            97

ARABELLA dips her finger in the cake and sucks it...

> ARABELLA
> Mmmm. I think I'll buy a whole college.

> JUDE
> You look cheerful in black.

> ARABELLA
> And rich. My poor friend died and left me everything. Where's
> my boy Jude?

LITTLE JUDE is playing with his SISTER in the distance, carrying her on his shoulders...

ARABELLA stares at him...

SUE looks pale with anger...

> JUDE
> Sue is his mother now.

> ARABELLA
> I'm not going to steal him away from you.

ARABELLA looks away from the boy wistfully and then at SUE...

> ARABELLA
> I see you've got another child on the way. Can you afford to
> look after mine?

> SUE
> What would you like?

> ARABELLA
> A very large slice please...

SUE takes the knife and starts to cut...

> ARABELLA
> Which is the college that refused you Jude?

> JUDE
> Bibbliol.

> ARABELLA
> Well I shan't have that on my dear.

ARABELLA pays JUDE...

> ARABELLA
> You were such a proud man Jude...

Revised 17.8.95

SUE hands her the slice of cake...

ARABELLA walks off towards LITTLE JUDE...   *

SUE looks like she's about to set off after ARABELLA...   *

JUDE stops her...   *

162A. EXT. KENNETBRIDGE FAIR. DAY.   NEW SCENE *

LITTLE JUDE stops suddenly as he sees ARABELLA...

ARABELLA offers him the slice of cake she's just bought...

                          LITTLE JUDE
            I've already had some thank you.

                          ARABELLA
            Maybe your sister would like some?

                          LITTLE JUDE
            She's too small.

                          ARABELLA
            How old are you?

                          LITTLE JUDE
            Twelve.

                          ARABELLA
            Twelve years and three months and six days. You see I
            remember exactly.

LITTLE JUDE smiles weakly...

                          ARABELLA
            Twelve was my favourite age. I used to do so many things
            when I was twelve.

LITTLE JUDE doesn't know what to say...

                          ARABELLA
            I bet you want to be thirteen though, don't you?

LITTLE JUDE smiles...

ARABELLA stares at her son...

There are tears in her eyes...

                          ARABELLA
            Do you have a wife yet?

LITTLE JUDE laughs...

                          LITTLE JUDE
            No.

Revised 17.8.95

ARABELLA

Then it'll be alright if I kiss you?

LITTLE JUDE

Yes.

ARABELLA bends down and kisses her son's cheeks and his forehead and his eyes...

163. INT. JUDE AND SUE'S HOUSE/ KENNETBRIDGE. DAY.

JUDE stares at the fire...

The embers glow. There is no more wood...

SUE

What is it?

JUDE

I want to go back to Christminster.

SUE

Because Arabella hurt your pride?

JUDE

Because I still have some pride.

SUE

Why do you care so much for Christminster? Christminster cares nothing for you.

JUDE

I can't help it. I love the place.

SUE smiles sadly and shrugs as if to say it's his decision...

99a

AT CHRISTMINSTER AGAIN

<u>164. EXT. REMEMBRANCE DAY PARADE/ CHRISTMINSTER. DAY.</u>

It's remembrance day and everyone is heading towards Church Street...

JUDE and SUE and the CHILDREN are caught in the crush of a slow moving CROWD. LITTLE JUDE holds his SISTER by the hand. JUDE holds their new born BABY in his arms. SUE has to shout over the din to be heard...

> SUE
> Did you know it was Remembrance day?

> JUDE
> I had a vague idea.

> SUE
> Who are we following?

> JUDE
> Everyone. We've all going to see the procession.

> SUE
> We have to find somewhere to stay?

> JUDE
> Don't worry...

<u>165. EXT. CHURCH STREET. DAY.</u>

JUDE squeezes his way through the assembled CROWD. He holds the BABY safely in his arms. SUE and LITTLE JUDE and his SISTER follow. JUDE finds a place for them all by the barrier...

JUDE points out the Wren Building to LITTLE JUDE...

> JUDE
> That's where the procession starts...

SUE is anxious to leave. The sky is darkening and there's a rumble of thunder...

> SUE
> Jude it's going to rain...

> JUDE
> They won't be long now.

JUDE's eyes are fixed on the Wren Building. SUE knows it's no use trying to persuade him to leave.

Suddenly JUDE feels a strong pair of arms grab him in a neck hold and push his face down...

> UNCLE JOE
> Guess who?

> JUDE
> I'd know that voice anywhere... Uncle Joe.

UNCLE JOE lets go of Jude and calls out across the crowd...

UNCLE JOE
Oi! Jim! Tinker Taylor! Over here! I've found the Tutor of St Slums College, Christminster!

TINKER TAYLOR and UNCLE JIM stumble over drunkenly...

TINKER TAYLOR
Can you still say the apostles creed in Latin?

TINKER TAYLOR offers JUDE his bottle of beer...

JUDE takes a swig and starts to recite in a slow growl...

JUDE
Credo in unum Deum, Patrem omnipotentem...

They laugh happily...

SUE looks disapproving...

UNCLE JIM
Look at you Fawley. You don't seem to have done any great things for yourself by going away...

TINKER TAYLOR
He's got himself some more mouths to feed.

JUDE
And what a joy it is. Sue you remember my friends don't you?...

SUE
Yes of course.

UNCLE JIM
So cousins do get married.

SUE smiles weakly...

JUDE
And here is little Jude, my eldest...

UNCLE JOE
What's wrong with you little man?

SUE
He's tired. Jude...

JUDE
We'll leave in a minute.

TINKER TAYLOR
We've been looking out for you in the Christminster parade every year.

UNCLE JOE
We never thought we'd find you in the crowd.

JUDE
Things turned out different.

UNCLE JOE
No regrets I hope?

JUDE
Some. It's a difficult question for any man to answer...
whether to follow his dreams no matter what... or to give in
slowly and let life lead him where it will...

TINKER TAYLOR
And which are you?

JUDE
When I first came here to Christminster I had a neat stock of
fixed opinions. Over the years they dropped away one by one.
Now the further I get, the less sure I am of anything...

UNCLE JIM
Hear, hear...

JUDE
"For who knoweth what is good for man in this life?"... "And
who can tell a man what shall be after him under the sun?"

TINKER TAYLOR cheers loudly...

UNCLE JOE looks at SUE with a happy smile...

TINKER TAYLOR
Your husband's worth a thousand University men.

SUE
I've been telling him that for years.

JUDE is on tiptoes trying to catch a last glimpse of the University procession...

[PROCESSION TO BE RE-WRITTEN]

Several carriages drive along Church Street. JUDE catches a glimpse of the UNIVERSITY MEN
in their bright red robes. He points them out to LITTLE JUDE...

JUDE
Those are the University teachers...

A peal of bells rings out. The procession is about to begin...

The CROWD pushes forward. EXCITED FACES appear at the windows above the street. JUDE
holds his ground...

Slowly the giant doors of the Wren Building creak open...

One by one the ANCIENT LOOKING DONS in their gold and red robes emerge from the dusky hall.

SUE watches JUDE. He stares in innocent wonder...

The procession looks like a slow march of the dead...

166. EXT. BOARDING HOUSE/ CHRISTMINSTER. DAY.

JUDE knocks on the boarding house door. The sound is drowned out by the rain. There's only room for SUE and the BABY under the umbrella. JUDE and LITTLE JUDE and his SISTER are drenched...

A sour looking OLD MAN opens his window above them. JUDE calls up...

                         JUDE
            We're looking for somewhere to stay.

                         OLD MAN
            I don't take children.

The rain batters down JUDE's face...

167. EXT. BOARDING HOUSES/ COLLEGE LANE. DAY.

The rain falls thickly, obscuring the view...

The boarding houses are darkened to gloom by the towering College walls...

JUDE and SUE and the CHILDREN are turned away yet again...

168. EXT. SMALL BOARDING HOUSE/ SLUMS OF BEERSHEBA. NIGHT.

The ceaseless rain hammers down...

JUDE tries to hush the BABY. He rocks her in his arms. The child won't stop crying...

LITTLE JUDE holds his SISTER's hand...

SUE is bargaining with the ELDERLY LANDLADY...

169. INT. SMALL BOARDING HOUSE/ SLUMS OF BEERSHEBA. DAY.

LITTLE JUDE hangs his wet coat on the door of the closet room. He looks at his new home miserably. The walls and floorboards are stained with damp. There are no sheets on his mattress.

                         LITTLE JUDE
            I don't like it here.

                         SUE
            That's all there is.

Her tone is sharp. She takes out her frustration on the boy. LITTLE JUDE disappears back into the closet room...

                                    JUDE
                    I'll look for work tomorrow.

Outside the gutters flow with filth and water...

From downstairs there's the sound of a man shouting. JUDE and SUE can't make out the
words but they know the argument's about them...

                                    JUDE
                    How do they know?

                                    SUE
                    She asked me if we were husband and wife.

                                    JUDE
                    And you said we weren't...

                                    SUE
                    I couldn't lie.

                                    JUDE
                    Sue...

                                    SUE
                    It's nothing to be ashamed of. I won't hide it from anyone.

LITTLE JUDE emerges from the closet room again...

                                 LITTLE JUDE
                    Mother?

SUE ignores him...

                                    JUDE
                    What is it Juey?

                                 LITTLE JUDE
                    Nothing.

There's a knock on the door.

                                    SUE
                    It's open.

The LANDLADY walks in. She looks embarrassed...

                                  LANDLADY
                    The landlord's a bit unhappy about the little ones staying.

                                    SUE
                    We can't leave now. Not in this rain.

                                  LANDLADY
                    No dear I said that to him. Staying one night's fine.

                                      104

                                    SUE
                    But we agreed a week...

                                    JUDE
                    Thank you very much maam. We'll look for new lodgings first
                    thing in the morning.

The LANDLADY smiles awkwardly and leaves the room...

                                    SUE
                    Why do you give in?

                                    JUDE
                    What difference does it make?

LITTLE JUDE is still staring at SUE with big sad eyes...

                                    SUE
                    What is it now?

Tears start to well up in the boy's eyes. SUE feels guilty. She takes him in her arms and hugs
him...

170. INT. MAIN ROOM/BOARDING HOUSE. NIGHT.

JUDE and SUE are wide awake in bed...

The rain patters on the window...

                                    JUDE
                    We shouldn't have come back.

                                    SUE
                    It would have been the same anywhere else.

The bells of Christminster ring in the distance...

                                    JUDE
                    I love this place Sue. Even though I know it looks down on
                    people like me. The self taught. The too determined. It takes
                    two or three generations to do what I tried to do in one...
                    Maybe the boy will succeed...

She smiles sadly...

                                    SUE
                    You're still Joseph the dreamer of dreams. And a tragic Don
                    Quixote. And sometimes you're St Stephen, who sees Heaven
                    open up, even as they're stoning him.

JUDE smiles. He takes her in his arms...

There's a creak by the closet room. SUE sits up sharply. She can't see anything in the dark.

                                    LITTLE JUDE OFFSCREEN
                    I can't sleep.
                                    105

                                    SUE
                    Come and sleep with us.

LITTLE JUDE stays where he is. JUDE can just make out his outline in the dark...

                                    JUDE
                    What's wrong?

                              LITTLE JUDE
                    Is it because of me that we have to leave?

                                    SUE
                    No darling...

                              LITTLE JUDE
                    Then why do we have to move again?

                                    SUE
                    Because there's too many of us. There isn't enough room.

JUDE's eyes are getting used to the light. He begins to see the sad haunted look on the
little boy's face...

                                    JUDE
                    Come and sit here.

LITTLE JUDE doesn't move. He stares at them intensely. SUE feels uncomfortable under his
gaze...

                                    SUE
                    Go to bed now.

LITTLE JUDE stays where he is...

                                    SUE
                    I said go to bed.

Her tone is firm. LITTLE JUDE disappears into the darkness. They hear the closet door creak
shut behind him...

SUE feels guilty again...

                                    SUE
                    I'm sorry...

                                    JUDE
                    Don't worry. I'll go and talk to him.

JUDE gets out of bed...

                                    106

171. INT. THE CLOSET ROOM. NIGHT.

LITTLE JUDE watches over his BABY BROTHER and SISTER. They're asleep in their cots...

He hears JUDE come in but doesn't turn around...

JUDE kneels down beside him...

> JUDE
> What are you doing?

> LITTLE JUDE
> Watching them sleep.

> JUDE
> They love you very much Juey. You're their older brother. If they see that you're upset they get upset too. You have to be strong for them.

> LITTLE JUDE
> There's going to be another baby isn't there?

> JUDE
> Why do you say that?

LITTLE JUDE doesn't reply...

JUDE knows there's no point lying...

> JUDE
> You're right...

Still the boy won't speak...

> JUDE
> What do you want this time? A brother or a sister?

> LITTLE JUDE
> If there are too many children in the world why do people have more?

JUDE smiles gently. He finds it hard to answer...

> JUDE
> I don't know... Because they love each other or because they don't think... It just happens that way...

> LITTLE JUDE
> Mother said there were too many of us...

> JUDE
> She didn't mean you...

JUDE holds the boy's face to his chest...

JUDE
There aren't enough of you...

SUE watches them from the doorway...

JUDE smiles at her reassuringly...

172. EXT. STONEWORKS/ CHRISTMINSTER. DAY.

The STONEMASONS work in the pouring rain...

SUE watches JUDE talking to the FOREMAN in the distance...

JUDE shakes hands with the man and walks back. He slouches with his hands in his pockets...

SUE assumes the worst...

Suddenly JUDE punches his fist in the air. He's got his old job back...

SUE looks ecstatic...

173. INT. STREET IN BEERSHEBA. DAY.

JUDE and SUE walk arm in arm. They're in high spirits again, teasing each other happily...

SUE
I'm going to buy myself a dress with great big flowers, and flounces, and ribbons... And I need a hat.

JUDE
Of course you so.

SUE
With exotic plants growing out of it.

JUDE
I'm only getting twenty shillings a week.

SUE
It's a fortune.

SUE's like an excitable child. She almost bounces as she walks...

SUE
And then I'm going to buy a cake with six different layers of jam and cream.

JUDE
What about the rest of us?

SUE
You can eat beans.

174. INT. ENTRANCE TO THE BOARDING HOUSE. DAY.

The LANDLORD looks at SUE and JUDE coldly as they enter the boarding house. He's about to say something snide...

> SUE
> What's the matter with you?

The LANDLORD is taken aback by her directness. He's lost for words...

SUE walks primly past him, up the stairs...

JUDE tries to stop himself giggling...

They're like happy children...

175. INT. MAIN ROOM/ BOARDING HOUSE. DAY.

JUDE and SUE open the door, still sniggering...

The room is empty. The closet room door is closed. There's a creaking noise behind it, and a gently tapping...

SUE looks worried...

> JUDE
> They're still asleep...

SUE walks towards the closet room slowly...

There's a note on the floor...

SUE picks it up...

JUDE looks puzzled...

> JUDE
> What is it?

SUE doesn't reply. She hesitates at the door. The tapping sound is the noise of something bumping repeatedly against the door...

SUE can't go any further...

JUDE walks over...

> JUDE
> What's the matter?... Sue?

SUE doesn't say anything. She looks deathly pale...

JUDE walks past her and pushes the closet door. It won't open. It feels heavy...

SUE suddenly screams...

JUDE pushes the door open in panic...

176. INT. CLOSET ROOM. DAY.

A chair lies overturned on the floor. LITTLE JUDE hangs from a box cord tied to a beam. His feet swing gently against the door...

JUDE stares in horror...

The BABY BOY and GIRL lie lifeless in their cots...

Outside the door SUE starts screaming again...

JUDE gets up on the chair and cuts LITTLE JUDE down with a work knife. He works like an automaton. He can't hold the weight of the boy as the cord finally shreds. LITTLE JUDE falls out of his arms and crashes heavily to the floor...

177. INT. MAIN ROOM. DAY.

SUE is on her knees, her face buried in the floor, sobbing and convulsing hysterically...

178. INT. CLOSET ROOM. DAY.

JUDE holds his dead BABIES in his arms, trying to whisper them back to life...

179. MAIN ROOM. DAY.

SUE crawls on the floor, on her belly, writhing like a wounded animal...

180. INT. ANOTHER ROOM IN THE BOARDING HOUSE. DAY.

From the stairway there's the sound of hurried activity: footsteps running up and down, whispering voices, doors opening and closing...

JUDE and SUE stare at each other in silence...

There's a dragging noise outside. It sound like corpses being carried away...

JUDE starts to sob...

SUE stares emptily...

JUDE stops himself...

SUE's face is completely expressionless...

181. INT. MAIN ROOM/ BOARDING HOUSE. NIGHT.

JUDE opens the door for SUE...

She still has the same empty look on her face...

The LANDLADY is cleaning up the room for them. She sees SUE. All she can do is look sorry...

SUE looks right past her at the closet room door...

The LANDLADY has hung several items of clothing on the peg of the closet room door. SUE stares at the hanging clothes as if they were alive...

The LANDLADY realises her mistake and starts taking the clothes off the peg...

Suddenly SUE screams at her:

> SUE
> Leave them there! Leave them there!

The LANDLADY looks terrified. She walks out of the room quickly...

SUE stares at the hanging clothes...

182. INT. ROOM/ BOARDING HOUSE. NIGHT.

SUE lies in bed. Her bed clothes are soaked with sweat. She talks to herself feverishly...

> SUE
> I incited him, I incited him. I told him there were too many of us. I told him the whole world was against us...

> JUDE
> No Sue...

> SUE
> My eyes are swollen. I can't see. I can't see... It's your fault Jude... Yours and mine. We loved each other too selfishly, we only ever thought of ourselves...

> JUDE
> Stop it.

> SUE
> We were happy... We had no right to be happy... They were my babies Jude... They were my babies...

JUDE looks at the DOCTOR. He prepares a tranquilliser...

183. EXT. GRAVEYARD/ BEERSHEBA. DAY.

The URCHINS of Beersheba perch on the graveyard walls...

A small cortege follows the three small coffins...

CURIOUS ONLOOKERS follow at a distance. They have gathered in the cemetery to catch a glimpse of the notorious funeral...

JUDE shields SUE with his coat...

SUE looks only at her own feet as she walks...

184. EXT. GRAVES. DAY.

The PRIEST's voice carries in the harsh wind...

> PRIEST
> ...For we are made a spectacle unto the world, and unto
> Angels, and to men...

JUDE looks at SUE...

Her head is still bowed, her eyes fixed on her mud caked shoes...

> PRIEST
> ...Even unto this present hour we both hunger and thirst and
> are naked and are buffeted and have no certain dwelling
> place...

JUDE stares at the three open holes in the ground...

He fights the tears...

> PRIEST
> ...Being reviled we bless, being persecuted we suffer it, being
> defamed we entreat...

SUE is still staring down at the ground...

Her arms hang limply by her side...

> PRIEST
> We are made as the filth of the world, and are the offscouring
> of all things unto this day...

JUDE tries to take SUE's hands...

As soon as their fingers touch SUE pulls away sharply...

> SUE
> Get off me!

The PRIEST continues as if nothing has happened...

> PRIEST
> I write not these things to shame you, but as my beloved sons
> to warn you...

SUE is looking back at her feet again...

185. EXT. GRAVES/ LATER. DAY.

With the base of his spade the GRAVEDIGGER flattens the earth...

The FUNERAL CONGREGATION begins to drift off...

SUE stares at the GRAVEDIGGER in silence...

                         JUDE
          Shall we go.

                         SUE
          I want to be alone.

                         JUDE
          Please Sue.

                         SUE
          I want to be alone with my children!

JUDE knows it's no use arguing...

                         JUDE
          I'll wait for you by the gates.

SUE doesn't reply...

She keeps staring at the GRAVEDIGGER...

186. EXT. GRAVEYARD. DAY.

JUDE keeps looking behind him as he walks away...

SUE is in exactly the same spot by the graves...

ARABELLA approaches from the gate...

JUDE walks towards her slowly...

They stop and stare at each other in silence...

JUDE finds it hard to look at her...

                         ARABELLA
          Make sure my son has a beautiful stone...

JUDE nods silently...

                         ARABELLA
          I should have kept him myself. I should have kept you too...
          None of this would have ever happened...

ARABELLA stares at JUDE...   *

                         ARABELLA
          Would it Jude?   *

                         JUDE
          I don't know...   *

JUDE still can't look at her...   *

                         ARABELLA
          If I'd have come back to you...   *
                              113

                         JUDE
          Arabella please.

There are tears of confusion in her eyes...

                         ARABELLA
          I thought about it...not every day...but I thought about it... Did
          you ever...

                         JUDE
          No.

JUDE looks at her for the first time...

                         ARABELLA
          Then it wasn't my fault?

                         JUDE
          It wasn't your fault at all.

He looks at her kindly...

She turns and walks away...

JUDE watches her disappear through the gates...

He turns and looks back at the graves...

SUE is still standing on the same spot, almost like a ghost...

SCENE 187 CUT

Revised 17.8.95

SUE lies in bed. JUDE strokes her hair. She keeps her back to him and her eyes hidden in the pillow...

                    JUDE
          Why won't you look at me?

She doesn't reply...

                    JUDE
          Sue?

                    SUE
          Because it's wrong.

JUDE pulls her towards him...

                    SUE
          It's wrong Jude. We have to be punished.

She stares at him with cold empty eyes...

                    JUDE
          Haven't we been punished enough?

                    JUDE
          Our love was wrong Jude. That's why the children died. We
          defied him and now he's punishing us...

                    JUDE
          Who?

                    SUE
          God.

                    JUDE
          God has nothing to do with it. You of all people know that.
          You taught me that.

                    SUE
          I was wrong.

                    JUDE
          And now you can see clearly? In this state?!

                    SUE
          Don't be impatient with me. I'm trying to explain things.

                    JUDE
          There's nothing to explain. It was a horrible accident. It was
          senseless circumstance...

                    SUE
          It was judgement.

                         JUDE
          On what? Why do you talk like this?... We've done nothing
          wrong... We've done nothing wrong Sue...

SUE stares at him in silence, as if she blames him, and hates him...

                         SUE
          We are made a spectacle unto the world, and unto Angels, and
          to men...

189. INT. BEDROOM. NIGHT.

JUDE wakes up with a start, as if out of a nightmare...

Sue's side of the bed is empty...

JUDE hears a creaking sound in the room...

His eyes move through he darkness until they find SUE...

She's on her knees in front of the wardrobe. She's pulling out her clothes as quietly as she
can, folding them into a suitcase...

JUDE stares at her in confusion...

SUE seems to be whispering something to herself...

                         JUDE
          Sue?

SUE stops whispering but doesn't reply...

                         JUDE
          Sue?

She carries on packing her suitcase...

JUDE watches her as if he's dreaming...

                         JUDE
          Sue please?

SUE gets up and walks towards the door with her suitcase...

JUDE gets out of bed and blocks her way...

                         JUDE
          Where are you going?

SUE tries to get round him...

                         JUDE
          Listen to me...

                         SUE
          You child killed mine...

                         115

Her eyes burn...

                          SUE
          Your child killed my babies...

Her voice is filled with cold fury...

                          SUE
          How can I listen to you? How can I look at you? How can I live
          with you?

JUDE is too stunned to speak...

                          SUE
          Now let me go.

JUDE moves out of her way. He looks dazed...

SUE opens the door...

                          JUDE
          Sue...

                          SUE
          Don't come near me.

She turns on him venomously...

Her eyes stop him in his tracks...

SUE closes the door and leaves...

JUDE listens to her footsteps disappear...

His eyes start to shine in the darkness as the tears come...

190. INT. CHURCH OF ST SILAS. DAY.

Singing voices fill the vast cathedral...

SUE's voice soars above the others...

He eyes are fixed intensely on the altar piece...

JUDE watches her from the back of the Cathedral hall...

191. EXT. CHRISTMINSTER STREET. DAY.

A light mist covers the narrow lane...

SUE's footsteps echo on the cobbled streets...

JUDE follows her at a distance, unseen...

192. EXT. CHURCH STREET/ CHRISTMINSTER. DAY.

SUE keeps walking...

JUDE almost loses her in the CROWD...

193. EXT. SUE'S LODGINGS. DAY.

JUDE stands staring at Sue's window...

The curtains are pulled shut...

JUDE looks still and ghostly...

The curtains never move...

194. EXT. SUE'S LODGINGS. NIGHT.

The gutter runs at JUDE's feet. He's coughing violently in the bitter cold...

His eyes never leave Sue's window...

The lights go off behind the closed curtains...

JUDE stands up expectantly...

A moment later the front door opens and SUE steps out...

She doesn't look in JUDE's direction...

She's dressed all in black...

She walks away quickly...

JUDE follows...

195. EXT. SLUMS OF BEERSHEBA. NIGHT.

The slums of Beersheba are lit by the vagrants' fires...

SHADOWY FACES stare up at JUDE as he hurries down the streets...

Up ahead SUE gives alms to the grasping BEGGARS...

JUDE keeps coughing...

196. EXT. CHURCH OF ST SILAS/ BEERSHEBA. NIGHT.

More firelight glows across the facade of St Silas...

JUDE stares at the building through feverish eyes...

197. INT. CHURCH OF ST SILAS/ BEERSHEBA. NIGHT.

JUDE pushes the heavy door open and enters...

The Church is dimly lit in candlelight and thick with incense...

High overhead a huge cross is suspended in the air by invisible wires...

It sways in a silent and barely perceptible motion...

Suddenly JUDE hears a faint noise of sobbing...

He looks around the smoky darkness...

Lying on the floor, by the altar, JUDE sees what looks like a bundle of black clothes...

> JUDE
> Sue?

At first there's no movement. Then slowly the bundle of black comes alive...

SUE looks up at him with haunted eyes...

> SUE
> What do you want with me? I want to be alone here. Why do you have to follow me?

SUE shivers in the dark...

> JUDE
> Sue come home.

> SUE
> I am home.

> JUDE
> You have nothing to repent.

> SUE
> You don't know my badness.

> JUDE
> Yes I do! Every atom and dreg of it. You make me hate Christianity and God and whatever has reduced you to this state...

> SUE
> It's right that I suffer...

> JUDE
> It's wrong. That a woman like you, should give up her mind, degrade herself...

> SUE
> Don't talk to me like that! I won't let you talk to me like that!

118

JUDE is stunned by her savage tone...

He stares at her in silence...

Slowly she calms down...

                    SUE
          I'm sorry. I'm sorry Jude...

                    JUDE
          I doesn't matter.

                    SUE
          No you have to listen to me...

                    JUDE
          Let's go home.

                    SUE
          No. Listen...

                    JUDE
          Sue...

                    SUE
          No I can't. I can't. I know what to do Jude. It's alright...

                    JUDE
          We'll talk in the morning.

                    SUE
          I have to go back to Richard in the morning.

JUDE stares at her in horror...

                    SUE
          You go too. Write to Arabella. Ask her to take you back.

                    JUDE
          But they mean nothing to us...

                    SUE
          We're still married to them.

                    JUDE
          No. You and I are married. You and I are married if ever two
          people were on this earth.

                    SUE
          But not in heaven... Not in this Church... I married Richard in a
          Church Jude...

                    JUDE
          With a piece of paper...

                              119

                          SUE
          I want to go back to him...

                          JUDE
          Do you care for him? Do you love him?

                          SUE
          I'll learn to love him...

                          JUDE
          But how can you? You love me Sue. You love me...

There is a long silence...

The cross creaks gently above them...

The rain patters on the roof above...

                          JUDE
          Say it...

She says nothing...

                          JUDE
          Say it Sue...

JUDE begs with his eyes...

                          SUE
          I don't love you anymore. I'll pray for us Jude.

                          JUDE
          Not for me.

JUDE turns and walks away...

He's still hoping that SUE will call him back...

She never speaks a word...

He keeps walking...

The cross sways in a barely perceptible motion...

JUDE flings the Church doors open...

<u>197A. EXT. SEVERAL MONTHS LATER/ CHRISTMINSTER. DAY.</u>

Gusts of snow blow at us...

Like travelling through a tunnel of smoke...

The bleak streets of Beersheba begin to emerge through the blizzard...

JUDE is walking away from his lodgings. We see a group of carol singers...

198. EXT. CHURCH STREET/ CHRISTMINSTER. NIGHT.

The cross of the martyrs glints on the pavement...

The fog drifts across the Building...

JUDE stares at the statues of the University luminaries, all along the stone walls...

A POLICEMAN walks over suspiciously...

                    POLICEMAN
          What are you looking at?

JUDE doesn't bother to turn around...

                    JUDE
          Them.

                    POLICEMAN
          I don't see then looking at you.

                    JUDE
          They're not. They're laughing at me.

                    POLICEMAN
          Move along now.

JUDE starts to cough painfully...

199. INT. JUDE'S LODGINGS/ CHRISTMINSTER. DAY.

JUDE leans over the edge of the bed, and wretches blood into a bowl.

His face is pale and craggy. The softness remains only in his eyes...

JUDE looks towards the window...

Snow covers the grim city suburbs...

JUDE reaches under his bed with difficulty and pulls out his boots...

JUDE stands in front of the mirror adjusting his suit and tie...

Every movement requires effort...

200. EXT. BEERSHEBA STREETS. DAY.

JUDE walks against the biting snow...

There are a few tatty signs of Christmas on the windows of the bleak Beersheba buildings...

JUDE keeps brushing the snow off his Sunday best...

201. EXT. GRAVEYARD. DAY.

JUDE walks through an avenue of trees...

The wind howls...

The snow blows in gusts...

Up ahead JUDE sees a lone figure at his children's graveside...

It's SUE...

She stands still under the spread of a snow covered tree...

202. EXT. UNDER THE TREE. DAY.

SUE hears footsteps in the snow and turns around sharply...

She looks dazed...

She stares at JUDE in confusion...

She tries to say something but the words won't come...

They stare at each other intensely...

Their eyes seem to take in every detail of each others faces, every change, every reminder...

>   SUE
> How did you know?

>   JUDE
> I didn't. I hoped. I thought it being Christmas and...

>   SUE
> My train leaves in an hour.

JUDE nods...

>   JUDE
> Where are you living now?

>   SUE
> Quite far.

>   JUDE
> You won't tell me where?

>   SUE
> You wouldn't know it.

>   JUDE
> I might find it.

JUDE smiles...

She doesn't respond...

                        SUE
        How are you?

                        JUDE
        Alright.

                        SUE
        You look well.

                        JUDE
        Do I?

SUE tries to smile...

There are tears in her eyes...

                        SUE
        I'd better go.

                        JUDE
        I'll follow you.

                        SUE
        No.

                        JUDE
        I won't stop trying. Even when you push me away. I promised
        you that.

For the briefest moment there's a glint of happiness in her eyes...

They stare at each other...

The snow drifts down all around their tree, cutting them off from the rest of the world...

                        SUE
        Jude... Please... Let me go...

                        JUDE
        Do you love me?

                        SUE
        Don't make me run away from you...

                        JUDE
        Do you still love me?

The snow blows all around them like a silver curtain...

                        SUE
        Please go away...

                         JUDE
          I will. I'll never come again if that's what you want... But I need
          to know...

SUE looks at him passionately...

                         SUE
          You've always known.

She moves towards him involuntarily...

                         JUDE
          Sue... I beg you... Come back with me...

                         SUE
          No Jude.

She takes him in her arms and kisses him on the lips. She keeps her mouth on his as if she
can't bear to ever let go. He body shakes gently as she sobs...

                         JUDE
          We are man and wife, if ever two people were in this world...

SUE pulls away from JUDE and runs into the snow...

JUDE lets her go.

His eyes fill with tears as her form melts into the snow...

SLOW FADE TO WHITE

CREDITS ROLL

Above: Jude leaves town
Top right: Phillotson leaves Christminster with a young Jude Fawley at his side.
Bottom right: Sue working as a sign writer.

Above: Sue.
Top right: Sue and Jude meet Arabella at the market.
Bottom right: Jude studying his books.

Above: Jude's childhood mentor, Phillotson.
Left: Sue and Jude *(above)* at the fair and *(below)* in bed.

Above: Jude working in the rain.
Top right: Sue and Jude meet in the graveyard.
Bottom right: Sue at the grave of her son.

CAST AND CREW CREDITS

POLYGRAM FILMED ENTERTAINMENT
presents
in association with BBC Films

A Revolution Films Production

A Michael Winterbottom Film

JUDE

starring

Christopher Eccleston
Kate Winslet
Liam Cunningham
Rachel Griffiths
June Whitfield

Cast

Jude Fawley	Christopher Eccleston	Gypsy Saleswoman	Amanda Ryan
Sue Bridehead	Kate Winslet	Curator	Vernon Dobtcheff
Phillotson	Liam Cunningham	Drunk Undergraduate	David Tennant
Arabella	Rachel Griffiths	Punter	Darren Tighe
Aunt Drusilla	June Whitfield	Mr Willis	Paul Copley
Little Jude	Ross Colvin Turnbull	Mr Biles	Ken Jones
Jude as a Boy	James Daley	Auctioneer	Roger Ashton Griffiths
Farmer Troutham	Berwick Kaler	Old Man	Raymond Ross
1st Stonemason	Sean McKenzie	Elderly Landlady	Freda Dowie
2nd Stonemason	Richard Albrecht	Priest	Dexter Fletcher
Anny	Caitlin Bossley	Politician	Moray Hunter
Sarah	Emma Turner	Blacksmith	Adrian Bower
Shopkeeper	Lorraine Hilton	Showman	Kerry Shale
Uncle Joe	James Nesbitt	Little Sister	Billie Dee Roberts
Tinker Taylor	Mark Lambert	Baby	Chantel Neary
Uncle Jim	Paul Bown	Newborn Baby	James Scanlon

Credits

Director	Michael Winterbottom	Production Assistant	Mat McHale
Producer	Andrew Eaton	Production Runner	Hannah Lewis
Associate Producer	Sheila Fraser Milne	3rd Assistant Director	Damian Wright
Executive Producers	Stewart Till	Floor Runner	Piers Thompson
	Mark Shivas	Location Contact (Scotland)	Cindy Thompson
Screenplay	Hossein Amini	London Locations	Roland Caine
	based on the novel	Location Assistant	Louise Mcmanus
	by Thomas Hardy	Crowd Assistant Directors	Elizabeth Binns
Director of Photography	Eduardo Serra A.F.C		Alison Goring
Editor	Trevor Waite		Celia Willett
Production Designer	Joseph Bennett	Stills Photographer	Joss Barrett
Costume Designer	Janty Yates		
Original Music	Adrian Johnston	Production Accountant	Con Cremins
Casting	Simone Ireland	Assistant Accountant	Debbie Moore
	Vanessa Pereira		
Stunt Co-Ordinator	Roy Alon	Dialogue Coach	Joan Washington
1st Assistant Director	Howard Arundel	Latin and Greek	Tim Carroll
2nd Assistant Directors	Matt Baker		Andrew Shackleton
	John Duthie		
Camera Operator	Philip Sindall	Art Director	Andrew Rothschild
Focus Puller	Simon Hume	Art Department Standby	Andy Nicholson
Clapper/Loader	Barney Davis	Graphic Designer	Frances Bennett
Camera Trainee	Danny Smith	Art Department Assistant	Tatiana Lund
Key Grips	Malcolm Smith	Art Director (Customs Hall)	Martyn John
	Gary Hutchings	Special Effects Supervisor	John Markwell
Steadicam Operators	Alf Tramontin	Special Effects Technician	John Dempsey
	Peter Robertson	Snow Effects	Dave Crownshaw
	Nigel Kirton		for Snow Business
	Vincent Mcgann	Technical Adviser (Stonemasonry)	Peter James
Sound Recordist	Martin Trevis	Set Decorator	Judy Farr
Boom Operator	Kate Morath	Props Buyer	Rebecca du Pont de Bie
1st Assistant Editor	Peter Christelis	Dressing Props	Mike Bartlett
2nd Assistant Editor	Joanne Harland		Colin Burgess
Supervising Sound Editor	Rupert Miles		Peter Bigg
Sound Editors	Kant Pan	Props Master	Paul Purdy
	Jeremy Child	Standby Prop Chargehand	Darren Reynolds
Dialogue Editor	Paul Conway	Standby Prop	Sean McConville
Footsteps Editor	Joe Gallagher		
Re-Recording Mixers	Robin O'Donoghue	Costume Supervisor	Jane Lewis
	Dominic Lester	Costume Mistress	Amanda Trewin
ADR/Foley Recording Mixer	John Bateman	Costume Master	Christian Motta
		Costume Assistants	Cathy Beaney
Location Manager	David Pinnington		Alan Graham
Unit Manager	Josh Dynevor		Ainslie Nimmo
Script Supervisor	Julie Robinson	Costume Trainee	Eleanor Appleby
Production Co-Ordinators	Ruth Coetzee	Make Up/Hair Designer	Mel Gibson
	Katie Drysdale	Make Up/Hair Supervisor	Amanda Warburton
Production Secretary	Ruth Hodgson	Hairdressing Supervisor (Extras)	Pam Haddock

Gaffer	Lee Walters	Focus Pullers	Peter Hughes
Best Boy	Gavin Walters		Tony Breeze
Electricians	Paul Sharp	Clapper/Loaders	Joseph Blackwell
	Matthew Moffatt		Steve Lawes
	Paul Harris	Grip	Richard Broome
	Matthew Butler	Location Manager	Garance Rawinsky
	Graham Cussel		
Generator Operator	Carl Mcgillvray	New Zealand Unit	For Barbara Williams Productions Ltd
Construction Manager	Steve Bohan	Production Manager	Barbara Williams
Studio Supervising Carpenter	Thomas Martin	Location Finder	Graham Sinclair
Location Supervising Carpenter	John O'Brien	Camera Operator	Roydan Johnson
Location Supervising Painter	Gary Crosby	Focus Puller	George Binnersley
Carpenters	Charlie Gaynor	Clapper Loader	Dean McCarroll
	Daniel O'Regan Snr	Key Grip	Tony Keddy
	James Henry	Grip Assistants	Sonny Parr
	Mark Brady		Damien Kwocksun
	John O'Regan	Boom Operator	Sam Spicer
	Robert Cann	Production Co-Ordinator	Elfriede Mowat
	Martin Freeman	Production Assistant	Debbie Alexander
	Peter Duffy	2nd Assistant Director	Emma Johns
Standby Carpenter	Daniel O'Regan Jnr	3rd Assistant Director	Stephanie Weststrate
Standy Painter	Ed Wolsencroft	Gaffer	Greg Nadler
Standby Stagehand	John Martin	Best Boy	Adrian Hebron
Standby Rigger	John Skinner	Generator Operator	John Hogan
Scenic Artists	Steve Mitchell	Electrician	Brendon Shadbolt
	Timna Woollard	Wardrobe Assistant	Diane Foothead
Painters	Dave Haberfield	Standby Prop	Anna Graves
	William Brown	Dressing Prop	Manu Sinclair
	Derek Walker	Props Buyer	Paul Dulieu
Plasterer	Charlie Green	Hair Stylist/Make Up Assistant	Yvonne Savage
Location Stagehands	Mark Goodman	Art Department Co-Ordinator	Ken Turner
	Jim Llewellyn	Stills Photographer	Pierre Vinet
Studio Stagehand	Derek Whorlow	Standby Construction	Martin Gorzeman
Riggers	Pat Hagerty	Set Carpenter	Ron Turner
	Denis Watson	Modeller	Adrian Landon-Lane
	Ted Hawkins	Scenic Artist	Jean Paul Eeckhoudt
	Ted Skinner	Scenic Artist Assistant	Gina Eeckhoudt
		Craft Services	Steve Couper
Unit Driver	Arthur Morrison	Location Catering	Flying Trestles
Camera Car Driver	Paul Mould	Helicopter Supplied by	Otago Helicopters
Props Drivers	Tony Rudd		
	Mick Crowley	Publicity	Charles Mcdonald for Mcdonald & Rutter
	Tony Knight		
Construction Driver	Bob Dean	Unit Publicist	Emma Davie
2nd Unit (UK)		Location Catering	Food for Thought
Camera Operators	Daf Hobson	London Catering	Set Meals
	Seamus Mcgarvey	Facility Vehicles	Dennis Diners SLV
	Andrew Speller	Film Processing by	Technicolor (London)
	Nick Beeks-Sanders		

Negative Cutting by. . . . . PNC

Originated on . . . . .Eastman Colour
Film from Kodak
Fujicolor

Camera/Grip Equipment . . . . . Panavision

Additional Grip Equipment . . . Grip House North

Lighting Equipment Supplied by Michael Samuelson
Lighting

Aerial Photography . . . . Hover-Cam Ltd

Title Design . . . . Frameline

Opticals . . . . Cine Image Film
Opticals Ltd

Digital Effects . . . . The Computer
Film Company

Post Production Facilities . . . . . Twickenham Film
Studios
Goldcrest Post
Production
Facilities Ltd

Editing Equipment by . . . . Salon

Digital Sound Editing by . . . . . The Sound Design
Company

Footsteps by . . . . Pauline Griffiths
and PJ's FTS &
FX Agency

Lawyer . . . . Jeremy Gawade.
Lee & Thompson
Solicitors

Bankers. . . . . Douglas Mason and
Nina Holmes for
Clydesdale Bank plc

Insurance . . . . Kevin O'Shea for
RHH Ruben

Completion Guarantor . . . . . . Film Finances Inc

Thanks to:

Reno Antoniades
George Carlaw
Ros Davies
Eddie Dyan
Graham Easton
Gerard Horan
Barry Kimm
Michael Samuelson
Roger Sapsford
David Wilder
Tate & Lyle Sugars
Scottish Historical Events Unit
Lothian Regional Council
Edinburgh District Council
St Giles Cathedral
The Signet Library
The Supreme Courts
Lothian and Borders Police
Lothian Regional Transport
Edinburgh and Lothian Screen Industries
Scottish Film Commission
Regent Inns Plc
Trustees of Blanchland Village
Blanchland Parish Council
Durham Cathedral
University Of Durham
Richmond District Council
The Cashmere Shop
Royal Mile Whiskeys
Royal Mile Curios
Robert Baillie Intl Newsagent
Lydbrook School (Gloucestershire)
St Mary The Virgin (Henley)
Sainsbury Homebase Ltd (Richmond)
London Borough Of Hackney (Press Department)

Special thanks to
at Polygram Film International:

Aline Perry
Jill Tandy
Jane Moore
Kathryn Smith

at BBC Films:

Stephanie Guerrasio
Geoffrey Paget
Gretta Finer

Filmed on Location in North Yorkshire, Northumberland, Durham, Edinburgh, London, New Zealand and at Twickenham Film Studios.

The characters and incidents portrayed and the names used herein are fictitious and any similarity to the name, character or history of any person is entirely coincidental and unintentional.

The motion picture is protected under laws of the United States and other countries. Any unauthorised reproduction, distribution or exhibition of this motion picture or any videotape version thereof or any part thereof (including the soundtrack) may result in severe civil and criminal penalties.